BThe reakthrough Factor

Creating Success
and Happiness
Through a Life
of Value

Henry Marsh

A Fireside Book
Published by Simon & Schuster

FIRESIDE
Rockefeller Center
1230 Avenue of the Americas
New York, NY 10020

First Fireside Edition 1998

FIRESIDE and colophon are registered trademarks
of Simon & Schuster Inc.

Designed by Elina Nudelman

Manufactured in the United States of America

10 9 8 7 6 5

The Library of Congress has cataloged the Simon & Schuster edition as follows:

Marsh, Henry (Henry D.).
The breakthrough factor: creating a life of value for success and happiness /
Henry Marsh.
p.   cm.
1. Success—Psychological aspects. 2. Values. I. Title.
BF637.S8M288   1997   97-12478   CIP
158.1—dc21
ISBN 0-684-81425-0
      0-684-84798-1 (pbk.)

Grateful acknowledgment is made to Russell & Volkening as agents for the
author for permission to reprint material excerpted from *The X Factor* by
George Plimpton. Copyright © 1995 by George Plimpton.

Acknowledgments

The concepts in this book come from the many people who have influenced my life. Foremost are my parents, who taught me, among other things, that you are nothing more than your life experiences and that you can accomplish anything if you put your mind to it.

Another big influence for this book has been my associates at Franklin Covey. I especially acknowledge Hyrum Smith for the support he has given me personally in addition to his support for this book. Others include Jerry Pulsipher and Kurt Hanks, who are credited with much of the development of the Franklin Covey Reality Model. Also contributing are many of the Franklin Covey consultants (Linda Eaton, Joe Smith, and Nancy Porthan) for their contributions and support.

Others who have contributed are Lee Benson and Tony Buzan. Lee was a tremendous help in writing and formatting the book. He quickly grasped the concepts and expeditiously made all the additions and revisions. It was always a delight working with Lee. Additionally, I credit Tony Buzan with much of the information regarding "imprinting" as applied to belief windows. Tony has done extensive work in researching how the brain operates, and I have become a fan of his work.

Finally, a heartfelt thanks to Jan Miller for her support and enthusiasm in making this book a reality and to Dominick Anfuso of Simon & Schuster for believing in this material.

This book is dedicated to James, Danielle, Andrew, and Lauren with the hope that the concepts presented herein will help you create a life of values for your success and happiness.

Contents

Contents

The Principle Made Me Do It!

There is an incredible power within each of us that is *the* way to achieving our personal best. It is the power of principles.

"It's the principle of the thing!" is a phrase that has been around our culture as long as anyone can remember. When all other reasons have been exhausted, it's the one given for continuing on. Beyond money, beyond power, beyond glory, even beyond winning, things are done simply "on principle."

Our principles make us do it.

This book is about principles. It's about what they are, how we get them, why we all have them, and what we use them for.

Most of all, it's about power. The incredible power of principles. A power so pervasive, so all encompassing, that there isn't anything any of us do that can't be traced back to its source. In short, our behavior *is* a reflection of the principles we choose to live by.

Some of us recognize and understand this power and use it for all it's worth. Others use it from time to time, but don't realize what it is they're using. And too often, many of us leave this source of power largely untapped in our lives, as if we had Michael Jordan on the team and kept him on the end of the bench.

This is *not* a book about morals. You'll find nothing here that preaches what values you ought to have; what you should believe. The focus is on recognizing that the beliefs we individually choose to live by are directly responsible for whatever quality of life we enjoy. There's just no getting around that. That's life! The key to enjoying peace, success, fulfillment, and contentment is putting in place those beliefs that will best produce those kinds of satisfying results. That's the challenge to each of us: to find out what beliefs allow us to realize our personal bests.

I use the phrase "personal best" because for thirteen years I competed in international athletics, and those were words I learned to greatly respect. I participated as a middle-distance runner on four United States Olympic teams. From 1977 through 1988 I was the top American in the 3,000-meter steeplechase—and now, in my "retirement," I check the results every new track season to see if, and when, the American record of 8:09.17 I set in 1985 will fall.

However, that American record was built upon an athletic career of personal bests. Every year I attempted to improve my personal best. That was my measuring stick. Was I running faster than ever before? And each year as I set new personal bests I felt great personal fulfillment. Early in my career, when I ran my fastest time, it was simply my own personal best—my own record. Later, when four of my personal bests were also American records, or American bests, they took on an added measure of notoriety. But those earlier "individual" personal bests brought the same satisfaction as the American personal bests that came later.

Personally, I can tell you that my entire experience as an athlete was an extremely satisfying "run," and I'm convinced it was because I had principles that allowed me to concentrate on striving for my own personal best, rather than worrying about someone else's personal best. Because of those inward-directed principles, I was not only able to compete for as long as I did, but I was able to thoroughly enjoy the experience.

Just as I sought to achieve personal bests athletically, we can seek to achieve personal bests in all areas of our lives. In this book, we'll learn how. Better yet, we can achieve personal bests well after our physio-logical peak, or age—which limits us athletically. We can have greater fulfillment every day we live upon the earth.

As a runner I happened to plug into the power of principles with-out consciously realizing what I was doing—and not only did that save my career in the beginning, it saved me from experiencing a lot of unnecessary grief during those times when things didn't go my way. Looking back, all I can say is thank goodness my focus was on "personal best" and not "gold medal."

I understand now why I didn't quit, and why others either wanted to, or did. I understand now why I was able to avoid the angst that can so often be an integral part of a career as competitive as interna-tional track and field. I understand now why I was able to deal with what the world would term "devastating setbacks." It was because I had my own finish line. I could "win" when others only saw losing. I had a different principle.

So I am evidence "Exhibit A" in the pages that follow. I use myself as a living example of one who has experienced the power of princi-ples in achieving one's personal best. It happened to me as a runner, and it happened to me again as an attorney. I graduated from law school, passed the bar exam, and began to practice law, all set to climb the legal ladder of fulfillment and success. But I discovered I was not cut out to spend my days in a law library, and I made a career change just when I was ready to cash in on all my years of preparation and training. In the pages that follow I detail the dynamics that caused that career change because they further help illustrate, and endorse, the power of applying beliefs that work for your own purposes. Not for anyone else's, but for your own.

I've been a few places and done a few things, and I've made some big principle-driven changes along the way that have made all the difference—and if it's true that you can't effectively sell something unless you believe in it wholeheartedly yourself, in the chapters to come you'll see I've taken care of that requirement.

Like many of us, I happened quite by chance upon the power of principle-driven behavior. But it doesn't need to happen that way. It is possible to become consciously aware of our beliefs and take care that they drive the kind of behavior that will produce the quality of life we're seeking. It's possible to realize going in that *our beliefs tell us what to do!* Once we understand that, we can start putting those beliefs in place that will tell us to have a peaceful, meangingful, enjoyable life—in other words, to achieve our personal best.

FORKS IN THE ROAD

A few years ago I saw a bumper sticker that read: GUNS DON'T KILL PEOPLE, PEOPLE KILL PEOPLE. I thought the point was well made. A gun is powerless until somebody decides to use it. A gun has no mind of its own; it can't make decisions. It is simply the extension of the behavior of the person using it, a whim at the beck and call of whoever's finger is on the trigger.

To illustrate the point, here are two names for you: Mahatma Gandhi and Adolf Hitler.

In many significant ways, these men were alike. By all accounts, they each had superior intelligence, excellent speaking skills, powers of persuasion, and the ability to inspire others to follow them and embrace their causes. They were goal setters. They had charisma. In short, they each had the qualities of leadership.

But despite their similarities, they couldn't have behaved much more differently.

Hitler's politics were fueled by beliefs of superiority. He believed in the supremacy of the Aryan race and acted accordingly. Armed with this belief, he was able to order the execution of millions of people and invade and dominate millions more. Gandhi, on the other hand, acted according to an entirely different set of beliefs, based on the sanctity of all human life. Because the Indian leader's aims were to improve the quality of life for his people, his behavior was on the other end of the spectrum from Hitler's. Whereas Hitler embraced violence, Gandhi eschewed it. One waged war. One waged peace.

Both behaved according to their personal truths—and that made all the difference.

IT'S THERE, MIGHT AS WELL USE IT

We all behave according to beliefs. We can't help it. We can't avoid it. There's no getting around it. It's a universal thing. It's like eating and sleeping. If we're alive, we do it. Whether we do it consciously or subconsciously, we all do it.

The simple act of breathing can actually help illustrate this distinction between conscious and subconscious action. Most of us go through our days breathing every few seconds and hardly give it a conscious thought. But those who understand the values of breathing *do* give it a conscious thought. Proper diaphragm breathing—inhaling deep into the diaphragm, or stomach, area to ensure a full exchange of oxygen and carbon dioxide—allows for better circulation, sharper instincts, and optimum coordination. Athletes learn *how* to breathe. So do dancers and performers and those who practice Yoga and other forms of meditation. Breathing, at its best, lets us fall to sleep, calms us down, makes us healthier, and helps us make free throws and perform a virtuoso *Swan Lake*. Breathing is in fact a tremendous power, *whether we realize it or not*. Some people use it as a power quite naturally. But most don't. Most have to either work at it, or they end up not getting the most out of something valuable that's completely available to them.

It's the same with principle-driven behavior. We are all driven by our beliefs, every last one of us. Our behavior unavoidably is a mirror image of our beliefs, but most of us are unaware of the power inherent in that natural resource. We use it unconsciously. We use it without even knowing it. We have the power of a Ferrari under the hood, and we barely touch the gas pedal.

To *really* tap into this power source—and, as a result, to achieve our personal best—we need to understand it, understand that we have it, and understand what to do with it.

Time and again, I have seen the importance of getting in touch with beliefs and the behavior that they drive. When that behavior delivers unsatisfactory results, it only makes sense that it ought to be changed, for the most basic of reasons: Who doesn't want to have satisfactory results in their lives? The only way to effectively change behavior is by changing the belief that's prompting it.

Through my involvement with Franklin Quest Company, now Franklin Covey Company, I have become an avid student, and ardent proponent, of seeking to achieve one's personal best through belief-driven behavior. It has not only become my life's work, but it's helped me to understand just how much more effective and valuable it is when it is understood. It's helped me realize that some of the belief changes I personally went through earlier in my life could have occurred much earlier—if I had known then what I know now.

I have seen countless people, many of whose stories are included in this book, who have benefited greatly by *consciously* seeking to better their lives through principle-driven behavior. The quality of their lives improved by first identifying their current beliefs, then recognizing the need to change the beliefs that were driving destructive behavior, and, finally, doing what was necessary to change them.

As with anything worthwhile, it's not always easy. Once in place, a belief—whether it's good for us or bad for us—can be mighty stubborn and difficult to budge. There are physiological factors at work, as well as psychological ones, that make us as loath to give up on a belief-in-place as we would a thousand-dollar bill.

UNWITTING ACCOMPLICES

We'll see in the following pages that too often we're unwitting accomplices in unproductive plots that undermine the quality of our own lives, plots that are usually entirely self-determined! We'll see that many of our beliefs were acquired in our youth, before we even realized what we were acquiring—and how, as a result, we can easily get caught up in unrelenting cycles of negative behavior that perpetuate the same unsatisfactory results.

We'll see the danger in short-term, diversionary remedies, modern-day "fixes" that don't get to the core of our problems, that don't really effect change, but only mask the pain—pain that is a direct result of not realizing our needs. We'll see how these short-term cures, which do nothing about changing our beliefs, can turn into addictions that are capable of further entrenching us in unwanted and unproductive patterns: addictions that range from drug dependence (legal and illegal) to oversleeping to shopping; addictions that contribute to the modern-day diseases such as most forms of hypertension, numerous forms of depression, and many other stress-related problems so prevalent in our society. We'll see how just coping with these diseases can occupy an enormous amount of time, energy, and expense and prevent us from building the kind of lives we really want by getting to the root of our behavior: our beliefs.

We'll explore the importance of having positive "self-talks," to maintain our newfound powers, and the importance of practicing preventive maintenance. We'll talk about the importance of being well-rounded and of getting in touch with what we want most—as opposed to what we want *now!* We'll examine the basic needs we all share and the way they unavoidably affect our satisfaction with life. We'll probe constructive ways to get beyond the static of daily life and understand what our beliefs really are; and how to begin to achieve our personal best by learning how to come up with our own theoretical new beliefs.

We'll explore control—not the need for it, but the need to understand it—the need to know what we can control and what we can't and act accordingly. There are no cure-alls to avoid hardships. Obstacles are a given. Life is not always fair, and even having correct beliefs in place won't change that. But having them in place puts life's obstacles in a perspective that makes them manageable. We can flow around them instead of constantly bumping into them head-on.

AN OWNER'S MANUAL

This book is about quality of life: an owner's manual on how to achieve our personal best in life, both personally and professionally, through principle-driven behavior. When we know what's driving us, then we're in a position to see if it will take us where we want to go. There are tips here to help us know—and, once we know, understand how to go about realizing our potential.

Principle-driven behavior is driven from within. The purpose of this book isn't to identify beliefs that are right or wrong. Instead, we'll identify beliefs that are either correct or incorrect, depending on the behavior they drive and the needs that are satisfied as a result.

It is within the reach of each of us, independently, to establish beliefs that are correct for us, beliefs that in turn will drive behavior that will produce satisfying results in our individual lives.

What do we really want? That's the universal question. Do we want to be a better salesman, a better husband or wife, a better parent, a better golfer or bowler, a better CEO, a better public speaker? Do we want to have better health, better security, a better feeling about ourselves?

I don't care what it is, we can achieve it by finding the correct belief.

We can search for our correct beliefs in a wide variety of places, both from within and without. People whose results we admire—and don't admire—whether we know them personally or not, from all walks of life, are fair game: from leaders of commerce and politics, from sports figures to coworkers, from our friends and neighbors to members of our own family. If we observe their behavior and find we would like to emulate it, then our task becomes a simple one of understanding the belief that drives that behavior and adopting it as one of our own. The opposite holds, too. Once we've identified them, we're also in a position to avoid the beliefs of those whose behavior we find harmful and unfulfilling.

The key is finding those beliefs, not merely observing behavior as is so often our natural tendency. Imitating may be the most sincere form of flattery, but it isn't the best way to achieve our personal best. When I was a teenager, I remember going to the movies and watching Robert Redford in *Jeremiah Johnson,* a movie about a mountain man. The lead character made a big impact on me. I liked his toughness, his ability to handle difficult situations. I left the theater deciding I would be like Jeremiah Johnson, and for a few days I acted like him, not saying much, holding a kind of steely stare—an impenetrable mountain man. But the impersonation, such as it was, soon passed. I returned to being me. In order to effectively behave like Jeremiah Johnson, I would have needed to get in touch with the beliefs that drove him. Since I wasn't willing to chuck everything I had, buy a mule, and head into the wilderness, I didn't have much of a chance to truly understand what those beliefs might have been.

I could have done that. If it had been important enough to me, if I had felt it would have greatly enhanced my quality of life, I could have headed for the hills.

TRUE FREEDOM

Beyond "borrowing" the beliefs we see and admire in others, it's when we objectively identify our own beliefs that we buy ourselves real freedom: true freedom that allows us to be in charge of ourselves; to not feel like we have to copy others or be slaves to conformity. When we know that we have the authority to alter those beliefs that bring us undue stress, unhappiness, pain, and sadness, that lower our quality of life—even if they might seem to work for others—we're in a position to truly chart our own course. We have ownership over ourselves.

In my days as a steeplechase runner, there was a time when I made a significant change in my training philosophy and technique, a change I was able to make only because of a new outlook I formed about my training principles. It had to do with my hurdling style. I had always gone off the same foot when jumping over a hurdle, just like everyone else. But I decided I wouldn't do that anymore. I decided I'd practice at being able to jump off either foot—because I felt that would work better for me. I could clear the hurdles wrong-footed. It was unorthodox. Nobody coached it that way at the time. Few ran that way. But I said, "So what?" and tried it anyway. The only reason I was able to do that was because I'd decided not to look at how others did it anymore. I'd adopted a new belief. It was that decision that freed me up to go ahead and be unconventional. And it did help. Without that change, and some others I'll talk about in detail later, I don't believe I'd have made my first Olympic team, let alone the other three. In short, I gave myself the freedom to chart my own course and achieve the best that was in me.

FEELINGS OF CONTROL

The power I stumbled onto and then tapped into that allowed me to dramatically improve was the very power this book is about: the power of achieving personal best through principle-driven behavior. I know firsthand that it is capable of bringing about truly dramatic results. I know it can result in feelings of personal control, self-management, contentment, and inner peace. Altering our beliefs—the way we look at life—really can facilitate significant change in meaning in our lives.

Whether we realize it or not, beliefs fuel us. They are what generate our actions or our inactions. They can propel us, thrust us, urge us on, catapult us, move us—choose your verb—and, conversely, they can inhibit us, freeze us up, delay us, and hold us back.

In *Webster's New World Dictionary* a principle is defined as "the ultimate source, origin, or cause of something," and "a fundamental truth, law, doctrine, or motivating force, upon which others are based."

In this book we will use Webster's definition of "principle" to see how our "personal truths" interact with "fundamental truths" or principles to forcefully motivate each of us. Since we form our personal truths based on what we believe will meet our needs, we will use the term "belief" interchangeably with "personal truth."

TIMELESS AND UNIVERSAL

It thrills me to realize that what first worked for me in college wasn't a quirk or a fluke, but a power that is both timeless and universal: the power of achieving personal best through principle-driven behavior. It's the same power that drove Benjamin Franklin to all his accomplishments more than 200 years ago (he understood it). It's the same power that can drive us all to the lives we'd like to have.

In the following pages we'll walk through the whys, the wherefores, and the how-tos of meaningful change. Together, we will uncover what truly motivates us, what drives us in our lives. We'll look at those things that produce the unhappinesses in our lives, as well as the happinesses, and realize just how much control we have over both areas.

In the book's first half we will look at a very powerful behavior model called the Franklin Covey Reality Model, a device that enables us to better see what drives us in our lives, what motivates us, and why we behave the way we do. As a visual tool, the Reality Model can help us see just how our beliefs, behavior, results, and needs are all interrelated. It helps us visualize how those things we learned in our early formative years are in fact powerfully driving us yet today. We'll realize that only by accurately identifying our true beliefs can we put ourselves in a position to change those beliefs that we discover aren't correct for our life's goals; and by changing those beliefs, we'll drive the behavior that will fulfill our potential.

We'll also look at the physical, mental, and emotional challenges that we all encounter, and we'll look at the importance of analyzing our actions "over time."

In the book's second half we'll look at specific steps we can take to achieve our personal best through principle-driven behavior. We'll look at things we can do to build ourselves up. We'll look at ways we can take control of those events that cause us anxiety and contribute to feelings of little or no control.

Most important, we'll look at time-proven ways to effectively form new correct beliefs and eliminate those incorrect beliefs that produce unproductive behavior, undesirable results, and feelings of despair in our lives. We'll look at the need to focus on what works for us—the need to focus on what will produce lives of contentment and inner peace. We'll learn how to take the theory outlined in the following pages and apply it in our lives so the theory becomes reality.

As I have traveled back and forth across America in my work, crisscrossing the nation from corporation to corporation, I have had a ringside seat, as it were, from which to observe people making dramatic improvements in their lives through principle-driven behavior. It's a thrilling sight. I'd like you to see those sights through my eyes.

You'll see I'm a big fan of achieving personal best through principle-driven behavior. I'm a recipient of the positive benefits myself, and I've seen many others benefit as well. This power we're about to explore has helped me appreciate the ability we all have to control our own lives, to become our best. It's a power that's helped me avoid a lot of negativity and has greatly enhanced my quality of life. For one thing, I know it helped me run faster. I know it can help you run faster, too.

Henry Marsh
August 1997

CHAPTER ONE

Principle-Driven Behavior: The Need-Belief Behavior Connection

An overview of the Reality Model, which diagrams the dynamics of human behavior, explains why we, and those around us, behave the way we do.

We all have them.

We all try to satisfy them.

They compel us, they prod us, they motivate us, they propel us, they steer us, they captivate us.

Twenty-four hours a day.

Every day.

Needs.

Needs are something the entire human family has in common. No matter where we live, how much we own, what language we speak, or the color of our skin, we're alike in that we all have needs: needs that drive our behavior and provide the basis and impetus for everything we do. It is the reality of needs that causes us to develop our personal truths in the first place.

Although as individuals we can be vastly different, our basic needs as human beings are nonetheless identical. They're the same for a billionaire on the Gold Coast of Long Island as they are for a beggar on the streets of Calcutta. There is no difference.

Many of us aren't even consciously aware exactly what these needs are. Sometimes it's not until we look backward that they come into clear focus.

In a survey conducted by Dr. Gerald Bell of the University of North Carolina, four thousand retired executives were asked this question: If you could live your life over, what would you do differently? Across the board their answers reflected a desire to take better ownership of their lives. In essence they responded that life isn't practice. Every day is the Super Bowl. It's the real thing.

These executives, all of them very successful by material standards, talked of taking better care of their health (not throwing away their health as if it were trash), spending more time with their families, spending more time with personal development or having more fun, paying more attention to spiritual development and community service. Give them another turn, and they displayed an overwhelming desire to take care of those things that, after seventy-plus years, they viewed as their most cherished and important values.

They were articulating their needs—and not what they may have once thought were their needs, but the ones they now *knew* were their needs.

THE FOUR BASIC NEEDS

Besides offering a perspective with the clarity of twenty-twenty hindsight, Dr. Bell's survey reaffirmed that as humans we are driven by four basic needs—needs that make up the quadrants of the Reality Model's Needs Wheel. (See illustration opposite.) After careful examination, it was determined that the desires of the retired executives, as for all of us, could clearly be assigned to one of these four basic need categories:

Needs Wheel

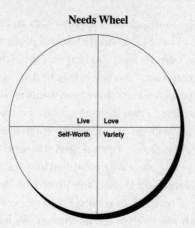

Live   Love

Self-Worth   Variety

The need to live
The need to love
The need for variety
The need for self-worth

Think of the things that are most important in your life—those things you desire most—and you'll find it's possible to fit all of them into one or all of the above categories: to live, to love, to have variety, and to enjoy a feeling of self-worth. These are the needs that drive our lives, all of our lives. Fulfilling them, or trying to, is what causes us to do the things we do. When we're successful at meeting these needs, life is satisfying; it's great to be alive; we have hope, enthusiasm, zest; we look forward to tomorrow.

When we're not successful—and it's amazing how out of sync we can get when even one of the four basic needs isn't taken care of—life is often just the opposite. It can be drudgery just to get out of bed and start the day.

One by one, let's look at our four common needs and define them further.

The first of these needs, the need to **live,** is basic physical survival.

To stay alive is the most primal of all the needs and the most enduring. It's the need to have food and shelter and protection from the elements so we don't die. It could also be described as the survival need. The common expression, "No one wants to die," is probably better said in its more positive form: "Everyone wants to live." As has been manifest over and over again throughout history, the desire to live is so strong that we will go to enormous lengths and spend great amounts of energy when our survival need is threatened. In primitive times, the need to live was easily identified and revealed in daily efforts such as finding food, shelter, and protection. In modern times, the need to live is revealed in such ways as our concern for our finances, our health, our clothes, and our homes. We have a need to feel comfortable and secure, to avoid as much as possible those dangers that threaten our ability simply to live.

The second need, the **love** need, is the desire we all have for intimate relationships. This is the need to have someone to watch a sunset or go to the opera with. In general, it's a social need. It's the need to share life with another. It's the need to love and be loved. We all have a need to belong, whether it's in our families, our work groups, our social clubs, or wherever. The love need is manifested in the time and energy we spend searching for, developing, and maintaining relationships with others.

The third need, the **variety** need, is the spice of life need. This is the desire for the things that make our lives fun and interesting. It's what we get excited and enthused about, what we choose to do in our spare time, what we find rewarding and fulfilling. We all have a strong need to be able to do different things and have plenty of options. We don't like to wear the same clothes every day, or eat the same lunch. We like variety. Sameness bores us. Even if we don't realize it, we go to great lengths to satisfy this need for variety. It's a major factor in our job selection. It is why people bungee jump, or sky dive, or collect stamps, or any of thousands of other things that bring diversity to life.

The fourth need, the **self-worth** need, is the one I think is the most compelling for us today. Our self-worth need is what gives meaning to our lives. It is who we are in the world we live in. This need encompasses religious convictions. It is also our need for self-esteem, for a feeling of acceptance, for a positive self-image. It's the way we look at ourselves and think of ourselves and the way we perceive that others look and think of us. We need to feel like we matter or we'll have no real incentive to live. This, I think, is especially true in our modern world, when we typically find ourselves with more discretionary time for social interchange. As with all of the needs, we will go to great lengths to satisfy our self-worth need. It has a tremendous influence on the kinds of cars we drive, the kinds of homes we live in, the kinds of jobs we choose, the clubs we join, the way we dress, and so on. Not feeling important can cause us to question the reason for living. A 1993 report said that 27 percent of America's high school students thought seriously about committing suicide. Why? Primarily, because their self-worth need was not being met.

These, then, are our needs categories. We all have them, and on a regular, if not daily, basis we spend our lives attempting to satisfy these four basic needs. Think about it. They are what drive us and motivate us in everything we do. A balanced life maintains all four needs with a measure of equality, thus producing a Needs Wheel that is well rounded (and, continuing the symbolism, gives us a smooth ride through life). An unbalanced life may overcompensate for one or two of the basic needs and neglect the others, or neglect all of them. The result is a Needs Wheel that is not fully round. In a worst-case scenario, unproductive, uninspired lives produce existences that are flat and don't roll at all. None of the needs are being satisfied. In a best-case scenario, all four needs areas are satisfied, and our lives, as a result, are productive, inspiring, and fulfilling.

Every day, meeting our needs, or trying to, is what we're all about. It stands to reason that all four needs require regular maintenance to be satisfied. They all require attention. When they're not satisfied, they'll cry out in any number of ways to get our attention. Sometimes we choose to listen. Sometimes we don't.

THE REALITY MODEL

If we agree that meeting those various needs to our own satisfaction is what will bring us the peace and contentment we want, it's important to understand the paths we take, consciously or subconsciously, in our effort to satisfy those needs.

This is where the Reality Model comes in. The model isn't complicated, and it doesn't offer any guarantees to a happy life. What it does offer is a kind of life blueprint that can help us see if our needs are being met, and if they're not, what ought to be altered so they can be met. The Reality Model is designed to help us see our own reality. By doing so, we can then better assess our beliefs and the behavior they drive. So, let's go through the model step by step.

THE BELIEF WINDOW

After beginning with your Needs Wheel, the Reality Model moves to what is called the Belief Window. (See illustration below.) Unlike the needs that are common to all of us, everyone has their own belief window. We're all issued our own when we're born. It's what each of us looks through to see the world. Each belief window is going to be unique—a one of a kind—and we look through it every day, all day long. Everything that happens, everything we experience, everything we see has to come in through our window. As it comes through the window we interpret it based on the beliefs we've established and built through our life experiences. Every new experience we have, we put another belief on our belief window and further affect its composition.

28

These beliefs become the "why" behind our behavior; they provide the power that drives what we do and how we act. We form these beliefs in an attempt to meet our needs. Based on our view, we establish our own personal beliefs. We can only see the world as we've experienced it, so it follows that it's our life's experiences that make up our frame of reference, our reality, our truth. And we write that truth in the form of beliefs on our belief window.

Belief windows and the beliefs on them are why we have different political parties, so many different religions, so many different biases and opinions, so many different viewpoints. We all have different experiences, so we all have different belief windows. You may want to look at it like a pair of glasses. We see the world based on what kind of prescription is on our glasses. It's our beliefs that create our prescriptions. Since we all have different sets of beliefs, like fingerprints, we're all going to have different prescriptions.

We're All Different

It's important to remember that it's our different experiences that create our different prescriptions, of course. If we're raised in Somalia, for instance, we'll see the world a lot differently than if we're raised in the United States. If we're raised Catholic we'll see the world a lot differently than if we're raised Jewish. If we're raised in a black community we'll see the world a lot differently than if we're raised in a white community. And if we're raised in an integrated community it would also cause us to see the world differently.

Not long after the fall of the Soviet Bloc I found myself in Eastern Europe, traveling through several of the countries that had emerged from Soviet communism and were now entering their free eras. In talking with the people in the midst of this transformation, I inquired as to their feelings on this change.

Being a true red-white-and-blue, apple-pie-eating, flag-saluting American, I fully anticipated a reply that went something like this:

"Freedom is wonderful. All our lives we dreamed of this day. Our prayers have been answered. Now we can travel as we please, do as we want, with no restrictions from the state. We can choose our job, we can choose where we want to live, we can vote for whomever we wish, we can read what we want, we can worship as we please, and we don't have to stand in any more lines unless we want to."

I'd based my expectations in large part on personal experiences I'd had with Iron Curtain athletes who expressed a desire to defect. I particularly remember a Hungarian athlete at a meet in West Germany clutching a miniature Statue of Liberty as if to say, "I want to defect."

What I expected, however, wasn't what I got.

I was surprised at the wariness with which most people were "embracing" their newfound freedom. Many of the older people longed for the "good old days" when they were told where to work, where to shop, where to live, where they could and could not go, and what to eat. For all of their lives, they had lived under a certain system, a system that, right or wrong, had been their lives. Embracing a new system was going to take a while. I heard several people say, "Freedom is overrated."

I was taken aback, of course. From my upbringing and my experience, I regarded freedom as more important than anything else. "Give me freedom or give me death." That was my prescription. I was surprised when I ran into people who had a prescription that in many ways was exactly the opposite.

Word Games

I've found that playing a word association game can help illustrate this point about different prescriptions on our belief windows. I'm going to give you a word and you blurt out whatever comes to your mind. Here's the word: "Toyota!"

Some of you will no doubt say, "oh what a feeling!" Others may say, "dumb foreign car." Others may say, "I love what you do for me!"

Still others may say, "quality" while others may say, "cheap car." Whatever your answer, it's a safe guess that it was based on your own personal experience with Toyota automobiles. If you have a relative who works for General Motors you may not be very fond of Toyotas, but if you have a relative who owns a Toyota dealership you probably think Toyotas are great.

The point is, we all see the same things, but we see them differently, depending on our life's experiences. That's the key. No two people have the same, exact life experience, and hence, no two people have the exact same beliefs. It's why one person can see abortion as murder and another person can see abortion as the mother's right to decide what goes on inside her body. They are conflicting beliefs, to be sure, but they're also different beliefs, each tied to what is written on a belief window. The beliefs on our belief windows become the "why" behind what we feel and what we do—in short, how we behave.

It's the wide variety of our prescriptions that makes our world the diverse place that it is. All kinds of people see all kinds of things differently. It's not so much what you're looking at as where you're coming from.

Fast Cars and Rules

To better understand how this concept works, imagine that you've just bought a new sports car, and you're out for a drive when you see a sign for a curve up ahead. Because you want to check out just how tight the steering is in your new car, you take the curve wide and fast. At about the same instant that you realize you can't hold the right lane at the speed you're going, you look up and see a big semitrailer truck coming into the curve from the opposite direction. It's coming right at you! The truck and your car are going to collide unless you do something fast. First you say, "Oh no, I'm going to die!" or something like that, and then, very quickly, you jerk your steering wheel to the left, slam on the brake, and roll over the embankment, narrowly avoiding the collision. The next thing you know the paramedics have pried you out of your car at the bottom of the ravine and taken you to the hospital, where they keep you overnight for observation and in the morning tell you you're banged and bruised a little, but you're going to be OK.

Now, let's run this imaginary experience through the Reality Model. First of all, which of the four basic needs was being threatened in this situation? Your need to live, right? Your basic I-want-to-survive need. Once the need you were trying to meet was established—and in this case it would have been established very quickly—then what principle was on your belief window concerning big trucks and little cars? Big trucks smash little cars, right?

That brings us to the third phase of the Reality Model. It's called the Rule phase. (See illustration opposite.) In this phase we apply a principle to any given event that is happening in our life. When an event comes through our belief window, we interpret it based upon our past experiences. Our rules surface in the form of "if" and "then" statements. In your sports car adventure, the rule you applied was "*If* big trucks smash little cars . . . *then* I'm going to die!" Rules might be thought of as mental responses to the application of our principles, and it's our mental responses, or self-talks, that trigger the fourth phase of the Reality Model—Behavior. (See adjoining illustration.)

Behavior

Remember what you did. First you said, "Oh no, I'm going to die!" Then you swerved and slammed on the brakes. Those were your actions; that was your behavior. Notice that you also had an emotional and a physical response *prior* to your behavior. Your emotional response was fear, panic, and anxiety. Your physical response was what was going on internally—the influx of adrenaline, the pounding of your heart, the sweating.

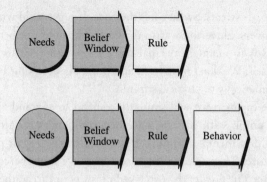

It was only *after* you experienced these mental, emotional, and physical responses that your hands jerked the steering wheel and your foot hit the brake. It was only then that you behaved. There will always be mental, emotional, and physical responses prior to our behaviors and actions.

It's important to note at this point that the intensity of mental, emotional, and physical responses is in direct proportion to the perception of what is happening. In this case, since the truck was big and time was of the essence, your mental, emotional, and physical responses were very intense. They screamed: "Do it now!" You responded in kind, in other words.

We never respond until we're compelled to respond. Our minds and bodies have an inherent natural tendency toward responses in kind, or to use the scientific term, toward homeostasis. Homeostasis is the tendency to maintain equilibrium, to stay in a like state. A good way to demonstrate homeostasis, and I often do this exercise in my work with corporations, is to have two people push against each other's hands. When one pushes hard, the other will push back hard. When one hardly pushes at all, the other will hardly push at all. Intuitively, both people are maintaining equilibrium, or homeostasis.

Our body's reactions to outside temperature changes also help illustrate this tendency toward homeostasis. If our body gets hot what does it do? It sweats. Sweat cools the body. If it gets cold what does it do? It shivers. Shivering warms the body. The objective behind both functions is to maintain normal body temperature, or to maintain homeostasis. We don't have to sit and think about it. Our bodies adjust automatically to physical stimuli.

In like manner, we will similarly respond to any and all outside mental stimuli with first mental, then emotional and physical responses. Most mental stimuli aren't as simple as a drop or rise in the temperature. They require interpretation—we must perceive what they mean. The greater the perceived pressure or threat, the stronger our mental, emotional, and physical responses are going to be. Unlike our body's natural response to, say, hot and cold, our response to life's daily events is based upon a perception that may or may not be a physical reality. The intensity of our responses will always be in direct proportion to our perception of the intensity of the threats (regardless of how great or small the reality). The greater the perception of a threat, the greater the response. Do you know anyone who overreacts? Why? Because the perception is greater than the reality. And to what is our perception anchored? Directly to our belief window, of course. The perception is always going to be based upon the beliefs that we've formed through our life's experiences.

CONSEQUENCES

This brings us to the final phase of the Reality Model—the Results phase. (See illustration opposite.) In the results phase we find out what the consequences are of our behaviors. Going back to the automobile accident, what were your consequences as a high-speed sports car driver who took the corner too fast? A trip to the hospital, medical bills, higher insurance rates, and you had to go out and buy another car, right? All those were results, or consequences, of the crash. But look at what else happened? You lived, that's what happened. That's the result we want to look at as we plug the hypothetical sports car experience into the Reality Model; that's the result we want to connect to the Needs Wheel in a Feedback loop. (See adjoining illustration.) Only by connecting our results to our needs are we able to accurately conclude whether the results of our behavior truly meet our needs. In the sports car example, the need that was being threatened was your need to live, and, since in the end you indeed lived, you satisfied your need. Since the results of your behavior satisfied your need, that means your belief, "Big trucks smash little cars," worked. It is, for you, a "correct" belief. You can safely make that determination. Making a hard left turn and crashing to the bottom of the hill was the right choice. It was preferable to a head-on collision with a big truck. However, notice there was also an incorrect belief at work here. Did speeding meet the driver's needs? No! The belief that it's OK to speed hurt the need to live because speeding unnecessarily cost the driver monetarily as well as physically. It's preferable to not have those expenses and injuries.

The exciting part about the Reality Model is that it can be applied to all areas of life. Through it we can identify those beliefs on our belief

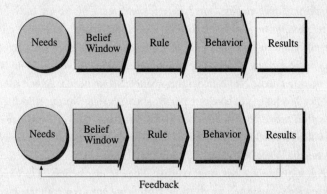

windows that drive the kind of behavior that produces results that satisfy our needs—beliefs that work for us. We can also identify those beliefs that drive behavior that doesn't work for us—in other words, behavior that produces results that do not satisfy our needs.

Laws to Live By

To help with that identifying process, there are two significant Natural Laws I want to share with you. By Natural Laws, I mean guiding principles that we can put in place that we know will drive productive behavior. Here are a couple of facetious examples: "Never fry bacon naked" and "Don't get in fights with ugly people—they have nothing to lose." The Golden Rule qualifies as a Natural Law—Do unto others as you would have others do unto you. That's just another example. You can call them truths or values or standards or words of wisdom, if you like. The point is, Natural Laws are *always* applicable.

The first Natural Law the reality model gives us is this:

> **When the results of my behavior meet my needs**
> **there is a correct belief on my belief window.**

It can be helpful if you circle the word "my" in this Natural Law. That's because we want to emphasize that we're talking about "my" behavior, "my" needs, "my" belief window. This is an individual thing. Everyone will have different personal truths. Personal truths are not good or bad. They're not right or wrong. They're correct or they're incorrect depending on whether they drive behavior that meets our needs. Not our neighbor's needs, *our* needs. As we use the Reality Model to analyze our personal truths, we want to find the beliefs that work for us, that are correct for us—and the only reason they'll be correct is if they drive behavior that meets our own individual needs. We'll be the only true judge of that.

Again, what are personal truths? They're our beliefs. They're the values we've assigned to all those things we come in contact with in our lives. They govern our actions. They are what motivate us and drive our behavior.

Let's use the telephone as an example. We probably all have some pretty definite beliefs on our belief window that drive how we behave on the telephone. This is particularly true in the workplace. Let's take the case of someone who is constantly annoyed when the telephone rings—and the reason for that annoyance and irritation is because there's a belief on the person's belief window that says, "Phone calls are interruptions. They get in the way of my productivity and therefore in the way of my success."

With that belief in place, let's start with when the phone rings and run this example through the Reality Model. What will be the behavior of the person who has a "phone calls are interruptions" belief on his or her belief window? We can easily imagine that behavior since we know it's going to be consistent with the belief. We can therefore imagine that typically it will involve short, curt responses and an unmistakable desire to end the phone call as soon as possible.

We can also safely imagine that such behavior might lead to rudeness, short-temperedness, and quite likely adversarial relationships with those unfortunate people on the other end of the phone line.

Now, by connecting these results back to the Needs Wheel we can determine if the need trying to be fulfilled is in fact being met. In this case, what need is driving the belief that "phone calls are interruptions"? Possible scenarios here are: 1) self-worth need—phone calls keep me from getting all my important work done so I don't look as good to my boss; 2) need to live—phone calls keep me from getting everything done, and I may lose my job as a result; 3) variety need—I don't have time to do all the fun things I want to do because phone calls take up so much of my time; or 4) love need—I don't have time for my family who needs me because phone calls take all my time. (Later in the book we'll go through a more systematic step-by-step process to show you how to determine which of your needs are being threatened.)

No matter which of the needs is most threatened, the question is, "Do the results of the behavior meet the need or needs?"

The answer in this case is quite obviously No. Rude behavior and adversarial relationships with others won't contribute to satisfying any need, let alone all of them. Since the results do not satisfy the needs, what does that say about the belief driving the behavior that produces those results? It is incorrect.

An incorrect belief should always be changed, of course, to a correct belief—to a belief that drives behavior that produces results that satisfy needs.

How about a new telephone belief that says, "Phone calls are interruptions, but they're *necessary* interruptions. They give me a chance to help others and at the same time increase my productivity"? With this new belief in place, it's easy to imagine resultant behavior that will include helpful and accommodating responses and a pleasant tone—the results of which will be attentive listening and a polite and courteous attitude. This doesn't mean that the person on the other end of the telephone couldn't be dealt with tactfully, or that there won't be occasions when a response such as, "I'm sorry, I'm on a deadline right now. Could I please return your call after lunch?" would be entirely appropriate. What it does mean is that the new belief will drive behavior that will create opportunities for increased productivity and better relationships with others—behavior that would in turn produce results that would potentially satisfy parts of all four needs.

We can, and should, put all of our beliefs to the reality test. Let's take another hypothetical example, and I'll use myself this time. In my line of work I'm on the road a lot, conducting seminars and giving speeches. I enjoy my work. Let's say that I have a belief on my belief window that says, "Henry, if you teach a great seminar or give a great speech, you deserve a reward." That's my truth. That's what I believe. Let's say I give my audience what I think is a terrific experience. I go back to my hotel room, and I say to myself, "Great job today. You deserve a reward." So I pick up the phone and say, "cheesecake please," and before long room service brings me a big piece of cheesecake with chocolate and strawberries on top. I eat that cheesecake and feel wonderful because I did a great job; now my hunger's satisfied, and I'm doing just fine.

The questions I have to ask myself as they relate to the first Natural Law are these: Is there a correct belief on my belief window? Did the results of my behavior meet my needs?

And the answer is . . . "I don't know yet."

It's too soon to tell. Yes, I'm comfortable right now, and my appetite is taken care of today. But I'll need to eat cheesecake every day for a year or more to really know if this behavior is meeting my needs.

Which brings us to our second Natural Law, which says:

Results take time to measure.

Do our results meet our needs *over time*? Is what we're doing a quick fix or is it a satisfying solution? Does it work over the long haul? As we observe our behavior, we don't want to focus on short-term isolated instances; we want to focus on our habitual responses, on satisfying a lasting need.

I remember making a conscious decision to cut down on my office hours when I began to ask myself this question: Ten years from now, what will I be glad I did today? Ask yourself that question, and you'll really begin to look at results over time, at the long-term impact of your behavior and not at short-term fixes. I remember that my ski days went up dramatically after I asked myself that "ten-year" question. So did my emphasis on my family, my work, my health, and all the other areas of my life I care most about. I was able to put office hours in proper perspective. I realized that I want to live life fully, and I want to have a lot of enriching and rewarding experiences. I started creating those experiences and taking advantage of opportunities, because I know I'm going to regret it if I don't. I planned trips with my children to have memorable experiences together. I got in the habit of finding out where they wanted to go, what their interests were, what they found important. I began to coordinate my business trips to also facilitate family outings. I realized my children will be grown and gone in a decade or so, and *now* is my only chance to build "bricks on the wall" with them. Further, I realized my need for variety. There were things I wanted to do in my life, and if I wasn't careful, the optimum time for doing them would pass me by.

Without plugging "over time" into my focus I wouldn't have planned trips that could satisfy so many of my needs or orchestrated any number of other experiences I determined to be important to me. Those two small words—"over time"—have the capability of giving us a new perspective on our lives, a perspective that enables us to put our priorities in their proper order. They are essential in helping us identify correct beliefs.

It's only when we view our actions in the context of the long run that we can enjoy all the benefits of perspective. Short-term solutions just won't do. It's long-term results that matter, and we'll have the patience to wait for them.

A Different Point of View

The life of Edward Joseph Flanagan serves as a good illustration of what I'm talking about. When he was a young priest, the Catholic church sent Flanagan far from his native land of Ireland to its archdiocese in Omaha, Nebraska. In Omaha, Flanagan became acquainted with several troubled youngsters. In deciding how best to deal with these boys, Flanagan determined that they could be rehabilitated if, instead of going off to a prisonlike facility, they could be raised in a community that taught them proper rules and values.

The priest had a belief that "There is no such thing as a bad boy."

In 1917 he boarded five of these juvenile delinquents in an old rundown house he rented in Omaha, where he allowed the boys to govern themselves. Over time, that rented house became a 1,300-acre community that gained its own incorporation. It was officially called Boys Town, and its founder, Father Flanagan, became its most famous resident—so famous that in 1938 the Hollywood movie *Boys Town* won a best acting Oscar for Spencer Tracy, who starred as Father Flanagan.

If Father Flanagan hadn't joined his principle—"There is no such thing as a bad boy"—with the perspective of "over time," Boys Town would never have happened. He chose to spend his time pursuing what he knew would bring him peace and satisfaction. He satisfied his needs and did a lot of boys a lot of good.

Looking Back Helps

Referring to the survey that began this chapter, you may find it interesting to know that none of the four thousand retired executives questioned said they wished they'd spent more time at the office. Not one! Their top two answers—1) making better use of your time through identifying values and goals and 2) taking better care of your health—also reflect the two nonrenewable assets we have in our lives (time and health). Once they are gone you can't get them back.

When you're seventy or on your deathbed, what will you wish you'd done? What beliefs will you wish you'd placed on your belief window? What needs will you wish you'd taken better care of? Start taking care of them now!

Instant Replay

Key Points

- We all have needs.

- Our needs fit into four categories—the need to live, to love, to have variety, and to feel self-worth.

- Our beliefs strive to satisfy our needs by the behavior they drive. Correct beliefs drive behavior that satisfactorily meets our needs over time. Incorrect beliefs drive behavior that does not satisfactorily meet our needs over time and keep us from reaching our personal best.

- The Reality Model provides a way to identify all of the above.

Personal Exercises

- Complete the Needs Assessment (see Appendix) to determine how you perceive what's going on in your life.

- Make a list of as many incorrect beliefs that you can recognize. We will work on these beliefs later in the book.

Where Do We Go from Here?

In chapter two, we'll look at how we get our personal truths and why our incorrect beliefs can be so hard to get rid of.

Blame It on Third Grade

Many of our principles are imprinted when we're still in grade school—and you thought you didn't learn anything in third grade! It's the third grader in us that is driving most areas of our lives today.

It sounds simple enough, this idea of achieving our personal best through principle-driven behavior. Plug in correct principles, behave accordingly, and Voilà! Our results meet our needs, and we live happily ever after.

Well, the truth is, it *is* that simple.

But it isn't that easy.

A lot of the reason is because of third grade.

I'm being facetious here, but only to a point, and only to make a point. I want you to think back to the third grade when the teacher gathered the whole class in a circle and announced it was time for art. I'm willing to wager that based on what happened there determined what you think of yourself as an artist to this day.

What happened probably went something like this: The teacher said, "OK class, everybody get out your crayons and drawing paper." So you got out your crayons and your drawing paper, and then the teacher said, "Here's a picture of a boat; everyone draw this boat." You finished drawing your boat, looked down at your boat, looked up at the teacher's boat, looked back down at your boat, looked at the teacher's boat again, and you thought, "Doesn't look like the teacher's boat . . . I can't draw!" Then your friends came by and looked at your boat, and they snickered and said, "Doesn't look like the teacher's boat," and you thought, "I can't draw!"

Then the teacher took all the boats and hung them up on the walls of the room. Every day for two weeks you got to walk in that room and see your boat, and every time you saw it you thought to yourself, "I can't draw! I wish the teacher would take the pictures down. I'm so embarrassed."

So I ask you today if you can draw, and you say, "No! You ought to see the boat I drew in the third grade. It stunk! I can't draw!"

And guess what? You never tried again. Why didn't you try again? Because through a traumatic experience one of your four basic needs was threatened when you were in the third grade, that's why. Which need was it? The self-worth need. You were embarrassed. You decided you could do without feeling that way in your life. You didn't want to be embarrassed any more. So whenever art came up after that, what did you do? You got out of it, or you hid your drawing, or you made fun of your drawing before everyone else could have the chance. Every time you did that you strengthened your belief that you couldn't draw! You made that belief stronger and stronger and stronger, and you've gone on strengthening it your whole life.

IMPRINTS AND SYNAPSES

Do you realize that in some very real ways, it's the third grader in you that's still driving you today? Is that a scary thought? The third grader in you drives you because you shaped your beliefs and your opinions and your perceptions of who you are back then. More important, from that day forward you have sought to validate your beliefs and experiences. It's your truth, your reality. It's your security blanket. In short, it is all you have. It's you! Life is a process of validating life's experiences and beliefs.

That makes it hard to change.

The strengthening of a belief such as "I can't draw" isn't just a figure of speech, either. It isn't wholly intangible. It is an actual physiological process that medical science calls imprinting. It's through imprinting that we record our beliefs, our life's experiences. We have five senses, and anytime one of those five senses brings in information, it's imprinted, or recorded, on the brain. This is done by a transmission through hundreds of millions of brain cells called neurons. Every time we have a thought, every time we have an experience, it's neurologically recorded between the neurons. Scientists have studied the process and have identified the spaces in which electrical/chemical signals pass. They're called synapses. We all have hundreds of millions of synapses that have been created to facilitate the need for neurological transfer.

Further, science tells us we all have the capacity to create new synapses for additional neurological transfers. The more experiences we have, the more synapses we bring into play; and the more we validate those experiences, the stronger the imprints become. In the third-grade art class example, the moment we compared our crummy boat with the teacher's terrific boat we created a synapse, or route, for an imprint to travel that said, "I can't draw!" Every time we looked at our boat after that or thought about our boat, we made our imprint stronger and stronger. We reinforced it. Much like constantly walking the same route in the mountains turns a path into a trail, so does our constant reinforcement turn our imprints into well-worn passages, and that translates to rock-solid beliefs. (Of course, I should note that I realize many have had experiences just the opposite. The teacher said, "You can draw!" and everyone admired your boat. To this day your imprint from that positive experience no doubt reinforces your art talent.)

WHY WE DO WHAT WE DO

In many instances, we may not even be consciously aware of the synapse trails that date back to our formative years. But rest assured they are firmly planted, well traveled, and in excellent working order.

The principles that created them in the first place are solidly on our belief windows. They shape the way we think and the way we see—and eventually the way we behave. They can be called up anytime, anywhere, through all the senses. Smelling creates powerful imprints. I remember walking through the streets of San Francisco recently, and as I passed by a corner market I smelled something that instantly put me in a good mood. It took me a moment to place the smell. Then I realized they were tuberoses. At my high school junior prom that's what I'd given my date, tuberoses. When I smelled them I was immediately back in Hawaii, at the high school prom.

It's difficult to underestimate the power of our early experiences, of what happened in third grade. I once met a lady who related during a seminar her own third-grade experience. She was in Germany as a young girl because her father was working there. She and her older brother were enrolled in a German school, where no English was spoken. Because the administration thought she was older than her brother, who was in second grade, she was put in the third grade instead of first grade.

So here she was, a first-grader in a third-grade class—where they spoke no English!

There was an assignment to copy material off the front chalkboard that she didn't understand. She didn't know what to do and struggled communicating with the German schoolteacher. As the teacher's frustration mounted, she finally rapped the little girl on the knuckles for not doing the assignment right.

The mix-up was soon discovered, and she was sent back to the first grade, where she belonged, but the memory of that experience was not erased. As an adult, this woman still admitted to a fear that she wouldn't perform correctly all the assignments of her job and would do something wrong. She was still being driven by that powerful imprint made when she was just starting elementary school.

TIME EQUALS STRENGTH

Over time, of course, our imprints—correct or incorrect—only get stronger, through validation. The stronger our beliefs become, the more powerfully they drive our thoughts and actions. Our behavior will reflect what we believe. Let's say by way of example that you were raised in a Republican family. Your dad was a Republican. Your mom was a Republican. Every time there was a presidential election they gathered you around the television and said, "I hope the Republicans win." They may have even had a sign in the front yard advocating a Republican candidate. All your life you heard them talk positively about the Republicans. So you have this belief that Republicans are good, and Democrats aren't so good. As you go out into the world you get some information that says the Republicans did something well, and what do you say to yourself? You say, "I knew it, that's what mom and dad said. Right on. Way to go. Republicans are good," and you strengthen, or validate, your imprint, your belief.

On the other hand, if you get some equally valid information that says the Democrats did something well, what do you say to yourself? You probably say, "It's a fluke. They're pulling the wool over my eyes. They didn't mean to do it." You discount it because Democrats doing well doesn't match with your reality, your truth, your experience. You push it aside. (Precisely the same process operates if we switch Republican bias to Democrat bias in this hypothetical situation.)

Over time, as two people validate their conflicting truths, they polarize or become further and further apart. They become entrenched in their beliefs. They only see what is true to them. They become blind to everything else. Do you know any hardheaded people? Why are they hardheaded? Because they've validated only their way and have been blind to everything else.

All of us, as members of the human family, not only have roots, but deep roots that drive our behavior because of conditions and events that may have occurred long before we were born.

The culture in which we are raised will unavoidably have a profound impact on how we believe—and behave. We readily adopt the truths of our culture and behave according to those beliefs. Just knowing this goes a long way in explaining human behavior.

STRONG ENOUGH TO DIE FOR

Consider, by way of example, the phenomenon of Japanese kamikaze pilots in World War II. Thousands of young Japanese airmen, many of them not yet twenty, joined the Kamikaze Corps toward the end of the war, when they were encouraged to do so by their leaders. Joining the Kamikaze Corps was the equivalent of signing your own death warrant. It meant that you'd climb into the cockpit of your single-seat fighter plane, usually a Japanese Zero, and purposely dive-bomb into an enemy gunboat in the Pacific Ocean.

More than fifteen hundred of these suicide missions were carried out, and nearly a hundred Allied ships were sunk, before the Japanese surrendered and the war was ended. In America, these suicide raids were unfathomable. But not in Japan. Because the age-old Japanese code of warfare viewed defeat as unthinkable and shameful, it made sense to pull out all the stops when subjugation appeared imminent. Suicide was seen as an acceptable weapon in the context of that culture. The name "kamikaze" was borrowed from a victorious chapter in Japan's military history—when the samurai warriors turned back invading Mongol troops in the late 1200s, the effort was aided greatly by what the Japanese believe were divine winds. The name they gave them was kamikaze winds. It was an honor to be a kamikaze pilot, and those who volunteered believed that by giving their life for their country they would have honor in their next life.

That's how strong our imprints can become, formed by the beliefs that drive them.

History is full of examples of unswerving devotion to cultural truths, just as it's full of unswerving devotion to truths that we acquire from other sources.

The point is, we're suited with our truths very early on, some of them even before we're born. They begin shaping us from childhood. We inherit them from our culture, our parents, our environment. Some we acquire ourselves. Whatever the source, the more reinforcement we give these beliefs, the stronger they become, and the stronger our synapses become.

I CAN RUN!

When I was young my development as a runner was based on a subconscious belief that could best be defined as "Winning beats sitting on the bench." Looking back, I realize that it was by following this belief that I wound up competing in a sport I otherwise might not have been attracted to.

Running was not my first sport of choice. I had grown up in Texas, and until I was fourteen years old I wasn't going to be the next Jim Ryun, I was going to be the next Roger Staubach. Football was king, and the Dallas Cowboys were royalty. In the ninth grade I was captain and quarterback of my junior high school football team in Richardson, a suburb of Dallas. Life might have been one long bed of roses after that except for one small problem: the 1968 season. The football team I quarterbacked didn't win a single game. We played ten games and lost them all. Still, I thought I was a pretty good quarterback who would only get better. In one game I completed all four of the four passes I threw. But my friends pointed out to me that three of them were to the other team.

When basketball season came along I played that sport, too. In the pecking order of Texas schoolboy sports, basketball ranked number three, right behind football and spring football. I had practiced jump shots in my driveway since I was a little kid, and I was deadly accurate, hence my assignment as captain and starting shooting guard on the ninth-grade team.

Then a truly unfortunate and, when you think about it, ironic event occurred in my life. You know how teenagers are prone to growth spurts that burst out of the blue, between dinner the night before and breakfast the next morning? Such a growth spurt hit me in late December of 1968. At the last basketball practice before Christmas break I was five-foot-four. At the first basketball practice after Christmas break I was five-foot-seven. Normally such an increase in height would be construed as the single greatest event in a basketball player's life. Now I could post up the five-four guys. But there was a catch. My shot was thrown completely off. I couldn't shoot the lights out anymore. Casting away with my combination throwing/shooting delivery was now sending the ball clanging hard off the glass. The good news was I was taller and stronger and in a position to become a better shooter once I adjusted and worked at it. The bad news was I wasn't starting any more. I went to the end of the bench and died there.

Which brought about . . . track season. I had never been anything other than average at the races we ran in gym classes, and the longest distance I'd ever run was 660 yards. There was no serious track and field background in my family, no foreshadowings of talent. In the aforementioned pecking order of Texas schoolboy sports, track and field checked in with a status just behind football and basketball. So as a fourteen-year-old I ran.

Wendell Harding, my junior high track coach, wasn't nicknamed the Drill Sargeant but he could have been. His idea of a good workout was two good workouts. He thrived on the sight of teenage bodies in various stages of collapse after repeat intervals and three-hour workouts. He set about whipping his teams into the best shape they could imagine (and in some cases that they couldn't imagine). If there was any talent anywhere, Coach Harding's philosophy was that it would come to the surface once you got all the rust out of the way. I remember only too well the ten-mile runs he'd put us through on the old dirt track behind our junior high school. I'd shower and limp home and be really sore and not sure if I wanted to do that again. Then the next day I'd do it again.

As a result, I discovered that I had an ability to run fairly fast for a fairly long time. By the time the Richardson School District finals came around that spring I entered the 1,320, a race just short of a mile, and, in addition to winning the race, I set a new district record. I had never been so thrilled—or rewarded—by anything I'd done in athletics in my young life. Everybody else came in behind me. The line formed behind Henry. It felt terrific.

My family moved from Dallas to Corpus Christi the next year, and what sports do you think I went out for at Corpus Christi King High School? Football and basketball? Hardly. I opted for the sports I had success in. I'd grown to really like winning. The first day of school I met with the track coach, James Blackwood, to plot my course of action for the year. I ran cross-country in the fall and was on the track team in the spring. What was the most fun wasn't nearly as important as what was the most successful. Think about it. What's more fun, shooting baskets or running laps? Trust me. Take my word for it. Shooting baskets is a lot more fun. In fact, what was the punishment for the basketball players who missed their baskets? Running laps, right. So what did I do? I went straight to the punishment. Why? Because I was the best at the punishment.

I was seventh in the Texas State cross-country championships as a sophomore, and in the mile at the state meet the following spring I was seventh again. We moved to Hawaii for my junior year of high school, and by now you couldn't have stopped me from running with all the surfboards on Waikiki Beach. Running fast was my ticket to self-esteem and popularity, to dates with good-looking girls, to trophies and ribbons and congratulatory pats on the back. That was my perception. That's what drove me.

I was fortunate to attend Punahou High School where, under the guidance of coach Al Rowan, I kept making improvements and beating people. After six state titles while in Hawaii, I got comfortable with what they call the "spoils of victory." I had plenty of imprints that said I was successful because of all the people who came in after I did at the end of a race.

SENILITY—THE ONLY WAY OUT

I'd developed all these imprints and their corresponding synapses that said, "Winning is number one." At the time, if I had known what a synapse was, I might have asked this key question: Once they've been made, can we get rid of our imprints? But sadly, I'd have learned that while the answer is "Yes, there is a way," it would not have been a satisfactory remedy. That's because the only way to get rid of our imprints is with senility. When a person goes senile the synapses that carry imprints actually break down.

So where does that leave us? If there's no other way we can break an imprint that's been strengthened and reinforced over a lifetime (and there isn't), how can we ever change our beliefs (and still keep our minds)?

Again, the answer is simple to understand . . . but hard to do.

The solution is to use a new synapse to make a new imprint. If I want to be a good artist after years of telling myself, "I can't draw!" then I have to form a new belief. I need to take art lessons. I need to *learn* to draw. I need to get in touch with the fundamentals. I need to practice and listen to teachers and fellow students who tell me I have the makings of a good artist. In short, I need to have new experiences. New experiences that reinforce my new belief. As I get better and better and as I listen to positive reinforcement, it's possible to establish a new imprint that is actually stronger than the old one. When that happens, and I'm asked if I can draw, I'll say, "Yeah, I can draw. You ought to see this house I just drew. Everybody liked it. I'm a good artist."

Likewise, if I want to be a runner who looks at his own results, and not the results of others, I need to keep saying, "Doing my best and giving my all is what's important," over and over again—until that imprint is stronger than the one that says, "Winning is the only thing."

Again, it won't be easy. We are a product of our life experiences, the sum total of our imprints, and most psychologists agree that by age five, or age seven at the latest, our personalities have largely been shaped. Our early imprints are our strongest imprints. That means that we're naturally going to perpetuate the beliefs of our parents and the third grade, for the rest of our lives—that is, unless and until those beliefs bring us too much pain. When the change looks less painful than the pain, *then* we'll seek out alternatives, but not until then.

Or—and this is an important distinction—we can recognize the ability we have to create new imprints that can overtake those old imprints we'd like to supplant—the ones that haven't been all that positive in our lives. We can do this *before* pain forces us to. Misery and suffering are not prerequisities to change. We don't have to hurt first. The pain doesn't have to get to the point that we consider it unbearable.

POSITIVE IMPRINTING

I should add here that many imprints are valuable. Many of them are keepers. We're lucky, of course, if our early lives were filled with positive imprinting. If our boat looked like the teacher's boat we could have saved a lot of time and energy.

I was lucky to have a lot of positive imprinting at a young age. I can remember my father going out of his way to give me experiences that would shape me and make me hungry for life. In the fourth grade I can vividly recall when he took me to Brazil. He was doing some work down there, and he took my brother and me with him. I remember going to the Copacabana and to the Iquacu Falls. My dad rented a plane with a friend so we could fly directly over the falls. When we came back we purposely took a flight that stopped in every central American country. Why? Because he wanted to give us that experience. I remember stopping at the Panama Canal, just so we could see it. He believed you're only as good and as rich as your experiences, and he passed that belief on to his family. It's been a positive imprint for me my entire life. That's one imprint, or a series of imprints, that I would never want to override.

I was also fortunate to grow up in an environment that stressed the importance of always being involved in a good cause. I've spent my life chasing goals. If it wasn't a gold medal or a law degree it was developing a seminar or trying to run a four-minute mile. The more I've learned about imprinting, the more I've analyzed why I'm the way I am—if anything, I'm an overachiever. I can trace it back to my parents, who always said that anything is possible. That was the family motto. They were the kind of parents who didn't act surprised if their kids got good grades. We didn't get rewarded for getting As in school.

There was this *expectation* of excellence, and that was what got imprinted. When I was young my mother gave me a quote from my grandfather, Henry D. Moyle, that I have always kept. He said: "You can accomplish anything of a righteous nature if you have the faith, the desire, and are willing to do the work."

CREATURES OF HABIT

When I look back on it further, my early experiences as a runner also help show just how strong our third-grade imprints can be, how they can relegate us to our places in life. I remember how easy it was, after a few races, to size up the field before a race and be able to predict fairly accurately where everyone would finish. We tended to be creatures of habit. So often, we'd mirror the results of our earlier races, myself included. I would finish in front of the people I always finished in front of, and in back of those I tended to finish in back of. Very often we pigeonhole ourselves because of our imprints. I'd look at a person I'd beaten in five straight races, and I had no problem at all thinking I would beat that person the next time we raced as well. But when it came to runners who had beaten me in the past, I had a lot of trouble thinking that this time the result would be different. I'd want the result to be different, of course, and I'd hope it would be different, but that's not what my imprint was screaming. My imprint said the results wouldn't be different, and often that would result in a self-fulfilling prophecy.

If we dwell on it, we can find many specific instances in our lives that gave us the beliefs that drive our behaviors. I remember working with a policewoman in one of my seminars who talked about her obsessiveness to overachieve. She took on an enormous number of projects in her life, and she had to be perfect at all of them. She expected nothing less of herself.

When I took her through the Reality Model and had her think about what life experiences she might have had that made her that way, she had an interesting response. She said both of her parents were alcoholics, who often ran away and abandoned her when she was young; they couldn't keep a job, and they failed at most everything they tried to do. She watched this as a child and developed a belief system that if you weren't perfect, that's how you'd turn out. That became the belief on her belief window. In response to that belief, she didn't just turn into an achiever, she turned into an overachiever. She would not let herself relax, ever. She was so afraid of failure that she became a perfectionist. That was her security blanket. With the help of the Reality Model, she was able to see that in order to take life easier, if she decided that was her goal, she would have to effect a change in her belief system, and to do that she'd have to create an abundance of new imprints.

THE ADVERTISING AGE

Another area that is responsible for a good deal of our imprinting, and one we're often not consciously aware of, is advertising. From an early age, we're susceptible to advertisements. We hear slogans, we see images, we hum jingles, we even smell perfume samples in magazines that come to our homes. Advertising is everywhere. Advertisers know what works; they know how to drive us. That's their business.

Well, this can be good, or it can be not so good. Advertising can give us imprints that are associated with correct beliefs—remember, correct beliefs are ones that meet our needs over time—or it can give us imprints that are associated with incorrect beliefs. We have to be careful. That's why getting in touch with our beliefs is so valuable. If we really know what drives us and where our imprints come from, we can keep the correct ones and discard the incorrect ones. Advertising is capable of generating positive behavior and results. Take Nike's slogan, "Just Do It," for example. It's not difficult to assume that that message is responsible for people reaching their goals and satisfying their self-worth need. Even if its original intent was just to sell shoes. "Just Do It" can inspire good imprints.

But advertising can be a double-edged sword. The same ads that inspired some youngsters to "Just Do It" and reach their athletic goals might have inspired other youngsters to rob and, in some instances, kill for the shoes being advertised. "Just Do It" might have had an entirely different imprint on these young people and driven entirely different behavior.

The point is, we are constantly being bombarded by imprint-making material, in one form or another. Once formed, the imprints create amazingly strong personal truths. We should take care to understand what those truths or beliefs are.

ACCURATE PREDICTIONS

Imprinting not only makes it possible for us to predict our own behavior well before an event occurs, but if we know what's on others' belief windows we can predict their behavior as well. In hiring new employees, companies that attempt to learn about the life experiences of prospective employees have an excellent chance of knowing what kind of employees they're getting. If you know what's important to a person, what they believe about things, what drives them, then it follows that you'll also develop excellent insight into how they're going to act. Their behavior is going to stay true to their imprints and their beliefs. They're going to act according to those life experiences that created those imprints.

On the other side of that coin, if you first observe a person's behavior patterns, you can go backward and fairly accurately predict what their beliefs are. It's behavior that provides us a view into a person's belief window and principles.

For example, if someone comes into a company with a history of jumping from company to company, you not only already know that that's his behavior pattern, but that it's following a belief because beliefs drive behavior. While you may not be able to completely define that person's belief without more insight, you can be reasonably sure that chances are good the behavior will continue. The jumping companies behavior will continue until there is a change of belief.

Behavior doesn't just happen. It's largely internally driven. External events don't have nearly the impact on behavior as imprints that have been established over long years of work and effort. Behavior perpetuates itself and will continue to perpetuate itself—unless and until there's a change in beliefs.

If someone with a history of getting along with coworkers everywhere they've worked applies for a job, you can be practically certain that they'll get along with coworkers at the next place they work. That's just another example in the workplace. Personnel directors could make their lives a lot easier by subscribing to that one standard.

Speaking of the corporate world, I've noticed that in many companies one of the chief concerns among employees has to do with bosses not treating them with what they perceive as respect. It's a very frustrating issue for a lot of people. If you think about it, it's not hard to predict what's on the belief window of bosses or supervisors who show little respect to those they supervise—even when you've never met them. They probably grew up in an environment where the be-lief was that bosses are supposed to be authoritative, hands-off super-visors. Bosses aren't supposed to get close to their employees or work directly with them. Their word is gold, their edicts are law, their commands supreme, that kind of thing.

It's quite possible this might have been learned from military ser-vice, or such beliefs might also have been learned in homes where men were kings who ruled the house. They got to delegate all the chores. They had little or no hands-on responsibility. That's the belief they grew up with. It's what they know. As a result, there's a lot of old-style management because that's the way a lot of bosses were raised.

Knowing this about your boss won't change your boss, but under-standing the imprints and the beliefs behind them can make for a lot healthier outlook than simple resentment.

Our imprints aren't just individual-oriented, either. Continuing in the corporate world for a minute, think about the beliefs people have about companies. There are beliefs about work ethic, dress standards, how often meetings should be held, acceptable limits of productivity, and who should park where. You name it. The list goes on and on. Some of these beliefs are in writing in company mission statements and employee manuals. But most are not. They belong to the area of "That's just the way things are done around here." Are they all true, and are they all healthy? Probably not. Some usually are, and in fact often most of these beliefs are good. But some might not be.

TAKING A CHANCE

A good example of this came from a training director I worked with who had a company belief firmly imprinted that said she worked till 6:30 every night because "that's the way things are done around here." Everyone else did, so she did, too.

Working that late caused her continual concern and distress because she had family needs that she knew were being neglected as a result. Her family needed her before 6:30. Finally, she came up with a new belief that said, essentially, "My work and my family have to be in better balance." To that end, she decided that she would work till 5:30 every night and then she would leave to take care of her family commitments.

With some fear and trepidation, she tried out her new belief. She would leave work at 5:30 and announce that she had family commitments. Do you know what happened? Nobody said a word. Nobody questioned her. She'd been driven by a perceived company belief that wasn't necessarily true. It turned out it wasn't written in stone. She believed she had to conform to it so she did. Reexamination allowed her to develop a new, and healthier, belief and imprint.

Understanding imprinting in the work place and the need to look at imprints that are being fueled by incorrect beliefs isn't only one-directional. Supervisors can benefit greatly from a clear comprehension of imprinting. In my work with Arby's, the fast food company, I have watched Steve Sparling, director of corporate training, use the Reality Model to look at employee beliefs that might be changed to make the managers, and in turn the stores, more productive. In one case, after noting that many managers had a tendency to take care of problems by fixing them themselves, he suggested to the supervisors that they should see themselves as being there not to help people do their jobs, but to support them.

Steve is a former weight-lifting champion, and he used weight lifting to help explain the difference between helping and supporting. If a weight lifter is trying for a new personal best in, say, the bench press, he never attempts more weight than he's previously lifted unless he has a person called a "spotter" who stands behind the bench. The spotter's purpose is to be there in case the weight lifter can't get the weight back to the bar. Spotters are essential, especially, as we might imagine, in the bench press. Otherwise, a weight lifter trying for a new personal best would have to be successful, or the bar would crush his or her chest and neck.

Steve said he'd never seen anyone even try to do their best lift without a spotter—for the simple reason that they wouldn't attempt to lift heavy weight without someone there to help out. For the same reason, he also said he'd never seen anyone find out their limits and set personal bests without a spotter. The spotter was essential. The spotter had to be there. But the spotter only acted as support. The spotter never got down on the bench and lifted anything until it was absolutely necessary. The spotter's job was to make sure the weight lifter could feel secure enough to go for his best.

Steve told Arby's managers that they need to be spotters, not lifters. To a lot of his managers that meant a new concept—a belief that says to truly be of assistance to others they need to be supporters, not helpers. They need to adopt an attitude that they'll jump in only when it's necessary, and then only as a support, not as someone who takes over and does the job. It's a new principle designed to drive an entirely different behavior, one that, over time, is designed to better meet the manager's needs as well as the needs of those being managed.

No Shortcuts

It's important to understand that developing new imprints takes time and attention. It requires patience. A decision to "turn over a new leaf" doesn't mean it can happen overnight. Nor will it happen merely by meditating or using some other Band-Aid approach. There are no shortcuts or quick fixes to finding new beliefs and building new imprints. Correct or incorrect, imprints need to be respected for the simple reason that they are there. They exist. They represent years and years of reinforcement.

Beliefs and imprints form the windows through which we view the world. This point was dramatically brought home to me after working with Sheila Holzworth of the Principal Financial Group in

Des Moines, Iowa. Sheila is a wonderful motivating trainer for Principal Financial. Sheila is also blind.

An accident at the age of ten robbed her of her sight, but Sheila was blessed with visionary parents who had prepared her well for the adversity that hit her at a young age. Being visually challenged did not deter her from striving for success and a rewarding life. Her parents, particularly her father, had instilled in Sheila a belief that if you think positively and always aim for the top, you'll get there. The adjustments she made after losing her eyesight meant changing some of her paths. But at the same time she took care not to eliminate any of her expectations. Her goals remained just as lofty as ever.

Sheila loved sports, but now, instead of participating in softball and gymnastics, her two favorite sports before her accident, she chose track. She concentrated specifically on the 100-yard dash—reasoning that a race consisting of one long straightaway was best suited to her capacity.

Sheila adjusted, but she did not change. Her imprints let her keep on "seeing." She lettered in track in high school and also in college, by which point she had added snow and water skiing to her athletic repertoire. In those sports she managed to go where no blind athlete had ever gone, winning numerous gold medals in national and international competitions while competing for the United States.

Another of this amazing woman's single achievements was when she became the first blind person to climb to the top of 14,410-foot Mount Rainier in Washington. For that accomplishment she was invited to the White House to be honored by President Ronald Reagan. Sheila's account of that climb to the top of Mount Rainier sounds very much like any other person's who has managed that considerable feat. "Believe me, the view from the summit was worth the effort," she told me. "It was a sunny day, the clouds were white and puffy, and the sky was a beautiful blue." She explained that two of her climbing companions who were deaf helped describe the scene to her. "But no one had to tell me how high I was," she said.

Sheila achieved her personal best because she was driven by correct beliefs. Having positive imprints allowed her to go on despite physical hardships and obstacles. In spite of her handicap, she is a person with uncommon vision.

Once we truly understand that beliefs drive behavior and that our beliefs are not of small construction but are the result of considerable imprinting, we can then appreciate the enormous work that has gone into building the framework that drives our actions and our attitudes. We can also appreciate why it requires considerable effort to achieve our personal best since we have to overcome imprints that have been around almost as long as we have.

Instant Replay

Key Points

- Imprinting is our brain's way of recording and storing our beliefs.

- Our personal truths are imprinted by five to seven years of age.

- The synapses created by imprinting are like old tires. They can't be destroyed. They can only be replaced by new ones.

- To achieve our personal best, we must overcome incorrect beliefs, many of which have been imprinted and reinforced ever since third grade.

Personal Exercise

Go back to your list of incorrect beliefs from chapter one and identify what life experiences created those beliefs.

Where Do We Go from Here?

In chapter three, I'll use a personal story to illustrate the power of imprinting and what it was that drove me to want to change an incorrect belief in order to achieve my personal best.

It Works!

I experienced the power of principle-driven behavior to achieve my personal best, and so can you!

I'd like to pause now and tell you a story—my story. It's about a time in my life when I was driven to change my beliefs—and about what drove me to want to make that change.

It all started the day I quit the college track team.

This was not front-page news. The public outcry was, shall we say, minimal. One gray day in January, after a workout that could best be described as uninspiring, I walked off the track and, with only myself as an audience, announced my "retirement" from the sport. That was that. There was no further discussion about the decision, or, I should add, any disagreement either. The next day, my first as a free man, I decided that my time would be better spent skiing than running.

At the time I was a rather pudgy, semi-out-of-shape twenty-one-year-old college sophomore at Brigham Young University in Provo, Utah. The way I saw it, my glory days of running were behind me. I was sure that's the way my track coaches (Sherald James and Clarence Robison) at Brigham Young saw it, too. Otherwise I would be on scholarship, which I most decidedly was not.

I ran the steeplechase, a 3,000-meter (approximately two miles) test of endurance around a track. The race includes thirty-five barriers (each three feet high), seven of which have twelve feet of water beyond them. The steeplechase has been described as the track event that most resembles a video game and also life, for that matter (with the obstacles). I hadn't run the steeplechase until my freshman season at BYU, when it became my fulltime event for one very good reason: Nobody else good was running it.

Coming out of high school I was a miler, aspiring to be the next Jim Ryun (possibly the greatest miler in history). And not without reason. At Punahou High School in Honolulu I was the Hawaii state champion twice and ran a 4:18 mile. Punahou named me its Athlete of the Year for 1972, and a number of colleges wrote me recruiting letters. BYU's offer appealed to me most since that's where my brother was attending and because the school is maintained and operated by the church to which I belong. BYU offered me a scholarship and a position on the cross-country and track teams, all of which I gladly accepted.

A NOBODY

I was just one of a crowd on the BYU track, and I soon realized that everybody there was a high school hero, too. Everybody had won his state meet, or placed really high, and many had won a few national meets for good measure. Talent, competitive drive, and high levels of confidence were everywhere: a whole lot of guys like me, in other words, only more so. I went through the usual freshman culture shock, realizing beating people was going to get harder and harder. I didn't even make the traveling squad for the cross-country team, and when track season rolled around I switched from one of the most popular events, the mile, to one of the most unpopular events, the steeplechase. The coaches thought the steeplechase would give me the opportunity for more success. So did I. But I still didn't letter.

After all that freshman-year indignity came the worst indignity of all—when the coaches encouraged me to interrupt my schooling to serve a two-year church mission. Serving missions isn't unusual for young men in the Mormon faith, in fact it is quite common, but in the early 1970s, the track coaches at BYU encouraged their best runners to serve their missions after they'd used up their four years of eligibility. They didn't want them to stop running for two years, at the same time piling on weight and a different attitude about sports. They worried that they might come back and not have the same competitive drive.

To me the coaches said, with enthusiasm, "So, Henry, when are you going on your mission?"

I TOOK A BREAK

I spent what could have been my sophomore and junior years in Brazil doing my voluntary missionary service. It was a wonderful experience, and I learned many valuable lessons that have served me well in many areas of my life and my worship of God ever since. I have never regretted my two-year "break" in Brazil. But it wasn't exactly high-intensity track training. For two years I rarely ran, except for the occasional sprint to catch the buses in Rio, and I took quite a liking to Brazilian cuisine. I returned to BYU twenty-five pounds heavier and not an inch taller.

I was still officially a member of the track team, but if I wanted my scholarship back I would have to re-earn it. That was the deal. It wasn't going to be easy because during my hiatus, two quality steeple-chasers had been brought in, one from Mexico and one from Norway. Both were on scholarship and both were faster than me. A lot faster than me. Their times were much lower than my lifetime bests.

I watched my new teammates/rivals in awe. They trained harder than I trained. They had better technique than me, and they both had a lot more experience. I was intimidated. I set about trying to compete with them by training the way they trained, and by doing my best to keep pace with their pace. To catch them I tried to copy them—and I wound up running into nothing but regular doses of discouragement.

What Was I Doing?

Then one day it hit me. Who was I fooling? What was I doing? I no longer had a scholarship. I was in an event behind two runners who did have scholarships and who took delight in beating me every time we trained. What's more, I was older than they were, and I weighed a lot more.

Running wasn't satisfying anymore, or much fun either.

So it was that on a nondescript weekday afternoon during the indoor season in January I walked away from the field house track and kept on walking, determined to enjoy my new lifestyle, which would include staying up as late as I wanted, eating whatever I wanted, skiing whenever I wanted, and playing intramural basketball.

This mood lasted for almost two weeks.

As I said, my departure from the track team was hardly headline news. No one, least of all the coaches, was even aware I had officially quit. For all they knew, I was still training the same as ever. Certainly, no one begged me to come back. No one asked me to reconsider. No one, that is, except for myself.

My parents had always made a point of stressing to my brothers and sisters and me that if you made a commitment then you saw it through to the end, even if the mood you were in when you made the commitment changed (make that *especially* if the mood you were in when you made the commitment changed). You didn't quit on yourself, in other words. So after I got a few late nights out of my system and a few ski days—strictly taboo for runners on the team—and after I played all the basketball I wanted, I realized I was having a problem facing myself squarely in the mirror.

One More Shot

I'd quit something I'd started, and I knew, instinctively, that if I didn't see the season through to the end I would regret it. I also knew, somehow, that just going back wouldn't be enough. If I didn't go back and give it my best shot I would still be disappointed. If I returned and did the best I could with what I had to work with and saw it through that way to the end, only then could I retire to the couch and the ski slopes with no arguments from within.

So I un-quit. I returned to the team (with the same commotion I'd caused when I left). But this time I had a different attitude. I decided that instead of worrying about how my teammates on scholarship were doing, instead of focusing on their every move and trying to copy their workouts, I would concentrate on getting the most out of myself. Whereas in the past I spent a lot of time wondering if my teammates were healthy, or if they were injured (or wishing they might get injured), or how fast they were running, now my focus was going to be on me. Was I healthy? Was I taking care of myself? Was I getting any faster? How was I doing?

I wasn't going to compare myself to anyone but me.

I became something of a maverick. I drew up my own workout schedules and set my own goals. Personal improvement was my new driving force. I lost weight. I became a toe runner instead of a heel runner like everybody else. I thought it might help. I ran on my toes for three miles, then four miles, then seven miles, and finally I could do a ten-mile run completely on my toes. I switched from high-mileage workouts to low-mileage workouts with an emphasis on quality, not quantity—because that seemed to suit me better. The high miles just wore me down. I learned to hurdle with either leg so I wouldn't have to stutter-step no matter how I approached the hurdles while running the steeplechase. That suited me, too. I experimented with a lot of things. Not everything I did worked, and I'd adjust often and sometimes get frustrated. But over time, through trial and error, I found what worked best for me.

That was January of 1976. Through the winter and early spring I trained with my head down, my eyes on no one else. Without races and without looking at my teammates, I had little idea of how much I was improving, but I was getting in better shape, I was sure of that, and I was enjoying my workouts a lot more.

I set a personal goal of running fast enough that spring to qualify for the NCAA national track-and-field championships scheduled for June in Philadelphia. I didn't care what anyone else ran. I wanted to run a steeplechase race in eight minutes and fifty-five seconds, the NCAA's national meet standard. That was my goal. It was something to shoot for: Philadelphia or bust; a tangible among all the intangibles; a faroff tangible, maybe, since the fastest steeplechase of my life had been run in nine minutes and twenty-five seconds three years ago when I was a freshman, but something to shoot for nonetheless.

A Real Eye-Opener

By the early part of April, after more than two months of straight training, I ran in my first steeplechase race in Tempe, Arizona, in a triangular meet with Arizona State and the University of New Mexico. As I toed the starting line, preparing to run my first competitive steeplechase in almost three years, I had high hopes, low expectations, and at least the knowledge that I'd worked hard to get here. I was off with the gun, my eyes on the track for all of the race's seven and a half laps. My determination was to run my own race and not react to what everyone else was doing. Starting slow was fine, it was part of my race strategy. My game plan was to rely on technique and a strong kick I hoped would be there for the final lap and straightaway.

When I finished and looked up at the clock I wondered if maybe I'd skipped a lap. My time was eight minutes and fifty-seven seconds.

I was surprised, and my coach was in shock. I had run almost half a minute faster—a relative eternity by steeplechase standards—than anytime in my life. What's more, if I could knock two seconds off that time in the next two months I could run in the national meet.

A month later I did better than that. At the Mt. SAC Relays in California I ran eight minutes and forty-three seconds and was in the NCAAs. Two weeks after that I ran eight minutes and forty-one seconds at the Modesto Relays and, in the process, set a new BYU school record. By early June I found myself at Franklin Field in Philadelphia for the NCAA finals race, lined up next to the prohibitive favorite, James Munyala of UTEP, a Kenyan with world-class credentials.

I almost won that race, losing at the tape to Munyala. My time was eight minutes and twenty-seven seconds. Not only did that make me, the guy without a scholarship, an All-American (the first of five All-America awards) and the fastest American in the NCAA meet, but the officials informed me that since my time was under the eight minute and thirty-two-second qualifying standard for the Olympic Trials scheduled later that month in Eugene, Oregon, I should consider myself officially invited to try out for the United States Olympic Team that would compete that summer in the Olympic Games in Montreal.

I ran another 8:27 at the Olympic Trials in Eugene and made the first of what would be four U.S. Olympic track-and-field teams. Barely five months had expired since I had quit the track team at Brigham Young, and I was on my way to the Olympic Games.

From those first Olympic Games in Montreal in 1976 through the 1988 Olympic Games that were held in Seoul, South Korea, I competed continually on the international track-and-field circuit. During my career I accumulated the second most world-ranking points in the history of the steeplechase. And I'm convinced I never would have even begun what turned out to be a thirteen-year competitive journey if I hadn't, in my own way, stumbled onto the power of principle-driven behavior.

MY NEW AND IMPROVED BEHAVIOR

When I changed my belief I changed my behavior—and my new behavior, unlike my previous behavior, produced results that met my needs.

My first belief was fine as long as I continued to beat other people. Basically, that *was* my truth—my self-worth was based on how many people I beat. If I beat the entire field, I was in good shape. If I didn't, my self-worth was in trouble. The only behavior that was acceptable was running faster than everyone else. The problem was that I couldn't control how fast everyone else was going to run—no more than I could control how hard they'd train.

It was only after I changed my belief from an external focus—beating others—to an internal focus that I was able to change my behavior. My new belief said that my self-worth was based on doing *my* best. I would compete only with myself. I exchanged an incorrect belief that had left me with very little control for a correct belief that left me with total control. I freed myself up so I didn't have to spend all my time worrying about others. I only had to worry about myself.

Essentially, I redefined my personal definition of winning—from beating others to getting the best out of myself. I did it by engaging the power of principle-driven behavior. At the time, I didn't articulate it that way, of course. I didn't even realize that's what I'd done. But I'd done it, nonetheless, and it changed me as a runner and a competitor. You could say it allowed me to give the proverbial 110 percent—since that's roughly how much my time improved that first year.

Besides allowing me to be the best I could be, my new belief and corresponding behavior gave me the power to be able to deal with not only the good results over that thirteen-year run, but also some results that, as far as the scoreboard was concerned, would prove to be more disappointing.

Instant Replay

Key Point

By changing my definition of "winning" I was able to keep running and discover my personal best.

Personal Exercise

Identify examples in your life where you made changes because your behavior wasn't working. What were the incorrect and subsequent correct beliefs behind the behaviors?

Where Do We Go from Here?

In chapter four, we'll look at pain and the key role it plays in determining what we do and when we do it.

When the Pain Is Great Enough

We live our lives to minimize short-term pain. But the incorrect beliefs that drive us are causing pain *today*. Why do we live with it? Because the pain of change is greater.

Knowing that my personality includes a good-sized dose of innate competitiveness—a condition no doubt exacerbated by my Texas roots—it still surprises me when I think back on my decision to walk away from the track team at BYU. I personally would have wagered that I never would have made that decision. I'd never have surrendered. I didn't think it was my makeup. But I did. I quit, at least for a short period of time, and further reflection has brought me to the conclusion that my change was proceeded by pain. When the pain got strong enough, I did something about it. I said "Enough!"

When all else is exhausted, pain is what motivates change.

Pain doesn't have to be physical to qualify, although physical pain is the easiest to understand. Make us walk over hot coals, put us on a medieval rack, or pry our fingernails off one by one, and we'll do whatever we can to put an end to the hurting. Give us a choice between a root canal with anesthetic or without, and that's no tough decision. What rational thinking person wants to physically hurt?

As it is with physical pain, when mental or emotional pain gets great enough, we'll also stop what we're doing. That kind of pain, despite being more difficult to quantify, can be equally intense, if not more so.

When the boss's demands get to be too much to handle, when the conflicts between family and work reach a level where no compromise is possible, when our work becomes unappreciated or so mundane we feel like screaming—we'll change. When the internal pain threshold hits its limit exactly as with physical pain, that's when we'll do anything within our power to make the pain stop. That's when we'll change.

No matter how great the cause or how strong the will, if our needs are not being met and a good deal of pain is being realized as a result, there will come a point when the alternatives will be looked at and turned to. We will eventually abandon our belief because of the pain.

THERE COMES A POINT

This concept was most dramatically demonstrated in perhaps the most notorious battle in American history, a battle that occurred in 1863 when the Civil War had a head-on collision in Gettysburg, Pennsylvania. The Union troops had the good fortune of arriving at the battleground just ahead of the Confederate troops and, as a result, were able to lay claim to the preferred high ground. The Confederate soldiers were thus left with two choices: Stay and fight and attempt to force the Union soldiers to retreat from their strongholds or retreat back to the South from where they came. They chose to stay and fight. Despite the high probability of heavy losses, they were convinced that their cause was just (and, some believed, divine). Further, they firmly believed that their leader, General Robert E. Lee, as beloved as any figure in military history, would not send them on a mission that was foolhardy, that they didn't have an excellent chance of winning. If he ordered them to fight, they would fight, and they were convinced that they would prevail.

So it was that when Lee directed General George E. Pickett to send his troops to attack the middle of the Union line on what would turn out to be the last day of the Battle of Gettysburg, Pickett complied. He didn't debate. He didn't question. He just went. With flags held high, the Confederate soldiers rushed in the direction of the Union entrenchments, storming toward the high ground of Cemetery Ridge across wide expanses of open meadows that offered little protection. The Union guns patiently waited until they came into range and then opened fire. Nearly twenty thousand Confederate soldiers would die that day in one of the most futile military assaults ever attempted.

The courage of those Rebel troops is talked about to this day, and a monument has been erected at Gettysburg to commemorate Pickett's Charge. Despite the fact the Confederate soldiers were well intentioned and believed wholeheartedly in their cause and in their leaders, and despite their uncommon courage, it's interesting to note that there came a point when they finally stopped fighting and retreated. However dedicated and zealous and convinced that right was on their side, even they did not go to the last man. When the pain got strong enough, they stopped.

Such examples of physical conflict can help make it easier for us to visualize the relationship between beliefs and behavior. In this case the Confederate soldiers, many of whom had never been in a losing battle up to that point in the Civil War, initially behaved according to two major beliefs—one that said they were fighting for a noble and just cause that could not be denied or defeated, and one that said their leaders were infallible and therefore incapable of sending them to defeat. Those were the deeply held beliefs that sent them into battle. Those were the beliefs that drove their behavior. (And, indeed, for the first two years of the Civil War they were beliefs that served them very well.) But the behavior was finally abandoned when it was overridden by pain. When forced by great pain and after their losses had piled up beyond human endurance, they adjusted those principles and changed their behavior.

In the final analysis, no matter how fiercely the Confederate army believed in its principles, in this case the principle acted on by the Union troops—never underestimate the value of the high ground—

ended up being the trump card. That was the correct belief in this situation.

Not Even George Was *That* Tough

Another example is the Muhammad Ali–George Foreman fight for the heavyweight boxing championship in 1974. In boxing annals this fight is a classic and for good reason. Going into the bout, Foreman was the reigning champion, and most experts felt he would be for a good long time. A giant of a man who had followed a gold medal performance in the 1968 Olympics with a meteoric professional career, Foreman was the prohibitive favorite against Ali, the former champion who, after a number of personal troubles, was trying to mount a comeback. Foreman was younger than Ali; he was bigger, stronger, and since he was the champ, he would have to be decisively beaten if the judges were to give away his crown. Going into that fight against the aging Ali, George Foreman was the epitome of confidence and youth, a supposedly unbeatable combination that had produced knockouts over the likes of former champions Joe Frazier and Ken Norton in previous title defenses. Foreman was confident. He was convinced he could overpower any man opposite him in a boxing ring.

Then the bout began and Muhammad Ali did a curious thing. He retreated to the ropes and covered his body with his hands and arms. Foreman, seeing what he believed to be a cowering, beaten man, obliged by flailing away with lefts and rights that came with dizzying speed and fury.

As the crowd winced, Ali just stood there. For seven rounds he stayed covered up, like a lighthouse being battered by a hurricane while Foreman banged away, sure that the next blow, or the next, would drop the contender to the canvas.

An interesting transformation began to take place as the rounds wore on. Slowly but surely, Foreman's blows began to lose their sting.

He was wearing out. He was running out of power. You could see it in the way he held his shoulders. As they began to droop his punches began to slow from what had been a steady unrelenting stream to a trickle. The strong man who was absolutely sure he could batter any opponent to the mat, and particularly one who wasn't fighting back, was running out of gas.

By round eight Foreman had nothing left. And Ali had plenty. The contender took over where Foreman left off, quickly winning by a knockout with a flurry of well-placed punches against a virtually powerless opponent. When the eighth round was finished, so was Foreman. The champ had been done in by subscribing to the belief that he could defeat any opponent by overpowering him. He stuck to that belief until it became obvious—painfully obvious—that there would be nights when that just wasn't going to work, and this was one of those nights. To be sure, for the rest of a career that would be long and successful (although the Ali bout would put it on hold for a time), George Foreman changed his beliefs—and, consequently, his behavior—so he would never again be done in by the strategy Muhammad Ali called the Rope-a-Dope.

I Know How It Feels

In my own way, I can relate to George Foreman's frustration, even if I've never been knocked out by Muhammad Ali. I too was a professional who executed behavior that I discovered over time wasn't working.

It was called practicing law.

As I've said, I have never been accused of not being a driven person. Striving to achieve is an asset (and usually, I believe, it *is* an asset) that my parents ingrained into me. It's made for a busy life, particularly so during my college-age years when I did my best to balance my competitive running career with my lifelong goal of becoming a lawyer. So it was that not long after competing in the 1976 Olympic

Games in Montreal I enrolled in law school at the University of Oregon in Eugene, a track-and-field hotbed where I could be assured of never having a minute to spare as I chased my dual priorities.

After graduating from law school I took a job with Parsons, Behle & Latimer, one of the largest legal firms in Salt Lake City, Utah. The firm put my name on its letterhead, gave me a wood-paneled office with a view, a secretary, a staff of paralegals, my personal code number for the copy machine, and directions to the library. In five years, if I kept up my billable hours and handled my caseload satisfactorily, I could be a partner. Five years after that I could potentially be a senior partner. I was on my way.

At first I was enthusiastic. As I said, entering the law had been a lifelong goal of mine. My father was a lawyer and so was my grandfather (whom I was named after) as well as my great grandfather. I thought practicing law was what I was supposed to do, what I was cut out to do. It was the cloth I was made of. I thought I had the genes for it.

Besides that and perhaps even more important, during my growing-up years I had been strongly influenced to become a lawyer because of the prestige that I perceived was associated with the profession. All my childhood inputs were that the law was a good profession and that lawyers were important. When people would ask me "What's your name and what do you do?" my belief was that by saying "I'm a lawyer" I would be important. In other words, my belief was that I'd only be as important and good as my profession and as others perceived the importance of that profession. A wholehearted belief in that personal truth made my decision to do what it took to graduate from law school and join a prestigious law firm an easy one.

But the more I practiced law the more I noticed a behavior pattern that was disturbing to me. Before long, every Wednesday became "hump day" for me. All I thought about during the early part of the week was how much I wanted to get over hump day and head for the weekend. Every Friday for me was T.G.I.F.—Thank Goodness It's Friday. I wanted the week to be over because I enjoyed what I did on the weekends a lot more than what I did during the week. As a result, the weekends flew by. I became a member of the weekday clock-watcher club, Monday through Friday.

Still, I persisted at my chosen profession, for a number of what I maintained (and still maintain to this day) were very good reasons. Money was one of them, and the prestige I felt I enjoyed because of what I was doing was another. I wanted my father to approve of me, of course, and there were many other factors. As time wore on and as the pain of practicing law became greater and greater for me—a pain that came from my needs not being satisfied—I started to reassess my reasons for being a lawyer. I rethought my personal truths.

THE LIGHT CAME ON

I began to think that maybe the most important thing about your profession isn't what other people think of you. The most important thing just might be to feel fulfilled and enjoy the day-to-day practice of your chosen profession. The law is a terrific profession if you're suited for it, like my father or, say, Clarence Darrow or Racehorse Haynes. But was I suited for it? I wondered. My personality thrives on being with people and on variety. I noticed that writing memos in the law office and doing research in the library didn't enthuse me like it did many of my colleagues. Preparing for trial didn't excite me as much as preparing for, say, a race on the track or one of my many opportunities to speak to groups about my Olympic experiences. Keeping billable hours and being in a fixed-time circumstance was stifling to me. The structure was constricting. A lot of people thrive on eight to five schedules, but I don't. I may travel and work fourteen-hour days, but it doesn't seem like it if I'm going somewhere and I'm not tied to a clock.

Over time, all of this became increasingly clear to me. As a result, my beliefs began to change. When the pain of practicing law became greater than the benefit of being able to tell people I practiced law, I altered my beliefs. My old belief was that my self-worth was based on how I perceived others viewed my profession. My new belief was that my self-worth was based on how much I enjoyed my profession.

I didn't execute this "replacing of beliefs" any more consciously in this instance than when I altered my beliefs as a college runner nearly ten years earlier. Then, as now, I reacted to the pain I was feeling, and that's what effected the change of beliefs.

A LIFETIME LEAVE

Acting on my new belief, in 1984 I took a leave of absence from Parsons, Behle & Latimer. I've been on that leave of absence ever since. I was determined to live by my new belief and to have my behavior reflect that new belief. As I left the firm, I was determined to feel fulfilled by my profession, even if I wasn't sure what it would be. I worked as a sportscaster for a period of time, and I started my own company called Athletes Unlimited. I was doing these things trying to find what really worked for me. I was actively seeking. Then I ran across the Franklin Quest Company in 1987, and I've been with them as a curriculum developer and motivational trainer for over ten years. That worked for me. I was happy to stay.

Not long after I started working for Franklin I realized what I'd been missing: There were no more hump days or T.G.I.F.'s. It didn't matter anymore what day of the week it was. I looked forward to Mondays as much as I looked forward to Saturdays. I felt satisfaction, enjoyment, and peace with what I was doing. The difference was tremendous. I had changed. The pain was gone.

Still, it was not an easy change. Replacing beliefs is rarely easy. When I left the legal profession I really struggled personally because I was changing beliefs that had been part of me practically my entire life. I wondered if my dad thought less of me than of my two brothers who were still practicing attorneys. I wondered if society would now perceive of me as less of a person if I wasn't practicing law. I wondered what the other attorneys thought. I really struggled with that. When I first started working with Franklin and people asked me what I did, I'd answer them with, "I'm an attorney, I work with Franklin." I answered that way because I was still tied into the belief that what people really thought of you was tied into what they thought of your profession (and besides, technically it was true, I was still an attorney). If I said I was an attorney I'd be well thought of. So I'd answer, "I'm an attorney, I work with Franklin." It took me a year and a half to overcome that—a year and a half of living the new principle before it became stronger and more persuasive than the old one—and I could say simply, "I work with Franklin."

After I left the law, I remember visiting Dallas, where my brother Will lived. I was passing through town, and I called him one evening and his wife answered. I said, "Is Will there?" and she said, "No, he's been working late every night on a big case." I remember thinking, "Gee, I'm glad I'm not doing that." I'm sure it was fine and satisfying for Will but it wouldn't have been fine for me. It wasn't that I wasn't working just as many hours. If you counted the nights away from home, I was actually working more hours than I had as a lawyer. But I wasn't counting the hours anymore, and that made a huge difference.

WHAT DAD THOUGHT

Not long after that visit to Dallas I was working with the space people at NASA, presenting a Franklin seminar, and I told them my story about my legal career. They asked me what my dad thought about my leaving the legal profession. I said I'd never asked him. They said ask him and report back. So I called Dad up that weekend, and I said, "Dad, NASA wants to know what you thought about my leaving the legal profession." You know what he said? He said, "Henry, when you left the legal profession I thought you'd thrown away your education." But then he added something that was very interesting to me. He said, "But I see now that you're probably doing more good for others than if you were practicing law."

I don't know if my dad just thought I was a bad attorney or what (and I didn't press the issue), but I came to realize through our talk that he wasn't a lawyer because others would think highly of him, and he'd never viewed me as a lawyer in that context either. The personal truths that had guided him and kept him in his chosen profession were different from the personal truths that had guided me to mine. He was a lawyer first and foremost to help other people. You don't tell my dad attorney jokes. He's real offended by them. To him the law is a service profession. That's how he sees himself as a lawyer, and that's how he saw me as a lawyer. If I wasn't going to serve others by practicing law it pleased him that I could serve others in another, perhaps even better, way.

What's pleased me—and him—is that I found a profession that's enabled me to feel a sense of self-worth based on my own personal enthusiasm and enjoyment of that profession and not on how I believe others perceive that profession. When I changed the belief that drove my behavior, I changed professions. It was that simple. Just as back in college I became a different runner when I changed my beliefs, I became a different professional when I changed my occupational beliefs from without to within.

THE PAIN MADE ME DO IT

In both cases, nothing would have happened if pain, in one or another of its many forms, hadn't ultimately gotten my attention. The pain in each case was different. The pain I felt as a runner was the pain of frustration of not getting where I wanted to go. I liked to run, I just didn't care for how it was making me feel. As a lawyer, the pain I felt wasn't out of frustration. To the contrary. I was prospering nicely as a barrister. I was making reasonbly good money and was generally well thought of in my firm. Professionally, I seemed to be cutting it. The pain I was feeling was out of dissatisfaction. I wasn't doing what suited my makeup, and I knew it.

Once the pain got great enough in both instances, I was motivated to make the necessary changes in beliefs to drive my behavior in new directions. In hindsight I can see that clearly now, and in my work I've been able to better understand the laws of cause and effect that were at work in my life even when I didn't know they were.

More important, I have been able to appreciate that it isn't necessary to see how much pain we can withstand before it's possible to change the incorrect beliefs that drive the behaviors that cause that pain. You don't need to do it my way. My way was the hard way. A clear understanding of the dynamics of principle-driven behavior can help us make corrections *before* the pain surfaces, let alone becomes intolerable.

Suffering is not a requirement, and while it's true that no one's life can be guaranteed free of discomfort all the time, it's also true that through the power of belief-driven behavior, casualties can be kept to a low minimum.

The best part is the choice is all ours, and it applies to all of our various situations. If something isn't working in our lives, and we're not sure why, a look at the belief that's driving our behavior can open vistas we've never before seen.

Instant Replay

Key Points

- When our needs are not being met, the result is pain.

- When the pain gets strong enough, we'll change.

- The pain doesn't have to get that strong. By getting in touch with our beliefs we can effect change that will considerably cut down on the suffering.

Personal Exercise

Make a list of recurrent situations in your life that cause pain (emotional as well as physical). Identify possible beliefs that are causing the pain and which needs are not being met.

Where Do We Go from Here?

In chapter five, we'll look at the very real physiological problems that are the direct result of incorrect beliefs and ways to avoid them.

Diseases of Choice

In the process of minimizing pain today, we form addictions. These addictions help us hide from our pain
and ignore the need to create new beliefs that can
get rid of the pain for good.

Right now you may be thinking, well, you'd have to be crazy not to
want to avoid all that pain. Who wouldn't want to change beliefs that
are incorrect? But wanting to and pulling it off aren't the same thing.
It's one thing to know you have what you need to storm the beach; it's
another to actually storm the beach. The reason can be summed up in
one word: obstacles.

Every day, all kinds of obstacles regularly appear in our path.
Their existence is a given; they're a part of life, and many of them are
so constant they're like clockwork. We can count on them. It's why
I've always paralleled running the steeplechase with running the race
of life. In both cases, just when you really get cruising, a hurdle ap-
pears. However, the steeplechase is easier than life. At least in the
steeplechase you know the obstacles are coming and that they're going to be in the same spot every time. That makes it a lot easier to prepare.

In life there's no way of knowing what's coming next or when.
Think of it, billions of belief windows, all of them different, coming
together every second of every day as we interrelate with one another.

That can be an exciting thought, or it can make you not want to get
out of bed in the morning. It depends on how you look at it. My ap-

proach to running the steeplechase taught me that. When I focused on everyone else in the race and worried about what they were going to do, the races weren't nearly as enticing and enjoyable to me as when I focused on how *I* was going to run the race and what *I* was going to do. That change in belief gave me an entirely different perspective on the exact same race. Everything was less imposing, obstacles included, when I focused only on those things I could personally manage.

CONTROL WHAT WE CAN

More than two hundred years ago, Benjamin Franklin was driven by the same realization. I think he articulated a Natural Law perfectly when he said:

While we may not be able to control all that happens to us, we can control what happens inside us.

That's the key: knowing what we can control (ourselves) and doing something about it. We can make our own choices. We get to choose how we react to all that happens to us.

Realizing the enormity of those things that can happen to us can be helpful in preparing for our reactions to them. If we sit down and make a list of the obstacles and hurdles present in our lives, it won't be long before the list is running off the end of the paper. A typical obstacles list for most of us would include such things as finances, family, workload, boss, traffic, relationships, deadlines, coworkers, mergers, change, and unreal expectations.

To our long list of obstacles we can add a second list, this one consisting of symptoms that are the result of those obstacles. This list will typically go off the page, too, including such symptoms as headaches, high blood pressure, ulcers, depression, anxiety, anger, nervousness, fatigue, twitching eyes, insomnia, illness, overeating, irritableness, helplessness, an overwhelmed feeling, and perhaps of most significance a barrage of negative self-talk. Notice these symptoms are physical, emotional, and mental in nature. They run the whole spectrum.

OBSTACLES AREN'T SYMPTOMS, AND VICE VERSA

Sometimes we confuse the symptoms with the obstacles. That's easy to do. How often do we hear people say, for example, that high blood pressure is their problem, when the reality is that it's their belief or perception about their demanding boss or their overbearing workload that is actually the source of their discontent and the cause of their high blood pressure. The boss is the obstacle. The high blood pressure is the symptom.

One of the saddest of our modern symptom diseases is anorexia nervosa. Medically speaking, anorexia nervosa is described as a psychosomatic disorder typified by self-starvation, which occurs most commonly among adolescent females.

Although this disorder was not as prevalent or as well known thirty years ago, it's now estimated that as many as 1 percent of young women in the United States are afflicted with anorexia nervosa. Ten percent of those who contract the disorder die because of it. Yet it is based primarily on a psychological perception the afflicted person has that she is much fatter than she really is.

This condition, the medical literature suggests, typically develops in connection with one or more of the following: a sudden move or change of environment, mental depression, peer pressure, and dysfunctional family life. As with high blood pressure, ulcers, the eating disorder bulimia (a purging disease that often goes hand in hand with anorexia nervosa), or any of the other ailments increasing in incidence in modern society, anorexia nervosa seems to qualify as a symptom. Like the others, it seems to owe its existence to the mental obstacles that bring it on.

STRESS IS A PERCEPTION

A popular modern label for these obstacles and their symptoms is stress. What, really, is stress? Let me offer this definition: Stress is simply our response to events we perceive as threatening to our needs. That's an important definition to remember, and it holds a key distinction. Stress is a *response* to what we perceive. It's our reaction. We own it. Whenever we perceive a threat to one of our four basic needs we will respond mentally, emotionally, and physically. Our response is what stress is all about. Stress is a response based upon a perception of a threat.

Statistics from the pain medication business paint a picture of modern stress that suggests its enormity and gives us insight into just how strongly we respond to what we see as our modern obstacles, or stressors.

In America alone, the over-the-counter pain medication industry does over $3 billion worth of business every year. That's how much Americans spend for nonprescription remedies to treat aches and pains, and that's not counting prescription drugs prescribed by doctors for more serious symptoms such as depression, high blood pressure, ulcers, and high cholesterol. Literally tens of millions of prescriptions are filled every year for these conditions. Drugs such as Prozac (used to treat depression) have become household names.

These conditions are costing corporate America billions of dollars every year. It is estimated that it costs corporations over $4,000 annually per employee for health care, and 75 percent of those costs are for so-called stress-related symptoms.

YOU ONLY CATCH THEM FROM YOURSELF

Now comes the multibillion-dollar question: How much control do we have over these symptoms?

The answer: nearly total control.

Except for certain genetic situations and bacterial-induced ulcers over which we obviously have no control and for which the above-mentioned drugs serve a valuable function, these are diseases of choice. They are self-induced. They are not contagious. You can't go home from work and say, "Dear, I shook hands with the boss today and picked up high blood pressure." Or, "Dear, I shook hands with a coworker today and picked up depression." A friend doesn't shake hands with you and pass on one of these symptoms. We give them to ourselves. Yet it's these symptoms that account for the majority of health and pain problems. That's right, the *majority*! They even make it much easier for us to catch bacterias and viruses that have nothing to do with the symptoms on our lists. They merely make us weak and more susceptible.

That's the bad news.

And also the good news.

If we can *choose* to have these symptoms, we can *choose* not to have them.

Let's take a look at traffic. Traffic is a good example, I think, because it's probably fair to assume that all of us have experienced some grief due to traffic hassles. It's a universal complaint, an across-the-board aggravation. Getting stuck in traffic, no matter how short the duration, no matter what kind of vehicle we're driving, is a waste of time; it keeps us from being productive or from getting to a meeting or home in time for dinner. Dealing with other drivers is a pain and road construction annoys us. Our tendency is to look at traffic as a necessary evil, sometimes even as a foe.

Let's change the setup. Let's say the next time you're in a traffic jam I will pay you one thousand dollars for every minute you're stuck in traffic. How will you respond? Of course the next time you're stuck in traffic you'll love it! You'll be courteous. You'll let everyone go ahead of you. You'll go out of your way to find problem roads. You won't care if you never get home.

Now, notice that the traffic did not change. It was the exact same event. What changed was your perception of that event. We took something we perceived as threatening, annoying, and challenging;

changed the scenario; and turned it into something we could actually look forward to. It was all based upon perception. That's all we changed; nothing more, nothing less. The traffic conditions weren't altered a bit. Instead of being uptight, anxious, and angry we were able to replace that with enthusiasm and excitement.

It's How We Choose to Look at It

Events, then, are not the problem. Perception is the problem. Attitude is the problem. How we choose to look at it is the problem. I like the story about the man standing in line to get his driver's license. After he arrives at the department of motor vehicles, he has to stand in the requisite multiple lines—standard procedure when your driver's license comes up for renewal.

But the more lines he stands in, the more agitated and anxious he becomes. His patience dwindles. He can't believe the time he's wasting. All the while, however, he can't help but notice that the lady in front of him seems totally nonplussed by the whole ridiculous time-consuming process. She's in a great mood. Line after line, hour after hour, she continues to smile. Obviously, she's enjoying the whole experience. Finally, by the last line, he just has to ask her. "This is really stressing me out, all these lines," he says, "and you're so happy. I've got to know why."

The lady answers, "Oh, I'm a professional line waiter. I'm being paid by someone to stand in line for them."

Remember, stress is how we respond to events based upon our perceptions. The problem for many of us today is that the way we're responding is killing us.

That is not an idle statement. It's not meant merely for shock value. Sadly, our responses often *are* killing us in a very real sense. A physiological understanding of exactly what happens when we create stress by our responses can be very instructive.

INTRODUCING UGH

First, let me introduce an old friend we'll call Ugh (see adjoining illustration). Notice that Ugh is making the acquaintance of a saber-toothed tiger. The tiger is Ugh's stone-age obstacle, and Ugh is exhibiting a stone-age response. Remember, our definition of stress is that it's a response to anything we perceive as threatening to our needs. Ugh perceives—and we have no problem assuming rightfully so—that the saber-toothed tiger is threatening his need to live.

Ugh

The tiger represents a sudden threat, and that triggers what we call an alarm response. That alarm response in turn sets into action an amazing number of physiological changes in his body. As soon as he sees the tiger (and simultaneously perceives the threat) Ugh's adrenal gland secretes a hormone we're all familiar with called adrenaline. Adrenaline, in turn, triggers chemical reactions in Ugh's body that empower him to run faster or fight harder, whichever he chooses, in order to hopefully survive the threat to his life. Very quickly, all kinds of things happen as adrenaline is sent through Ugh's body. For one thing, his blood pressure increases so his blood will move faster and get to Ugh's major muscle groups, which will be required for some major work whether his decision is to fight or to flee. As Ugh's heart beats faster, causing a rise in his blood pressure, and as the blood rushes to his major muscles, the circulation in Ugh's hands and feet slows down and his hands and feet, as a result, get cool. He doesn't need blood in his hands or feet right now; he needs it in his muscles, at the core of his body, and that's what his brain is telling his heart. Send the blood where it belongs. Now!

Meanwhile, while Ugh's blood pressure is rising, sugars and fats are being rushed into the blood stream. This is so Ugh will have plenty of fuel for his muscles. He'll have a sudden burst of energy when he needs it; he'll have power. As the sugars and fats rush to the muscles, his digestion becomes acidic because the blood is leaving the stomach, again for the major muscles, and what's left in the stomach are the acids and juices. These acids and juices will produce what Ugh will later describe as a knot in his stomach. Like his cold hands and feet, the knot in his stomach is an indication that he is responding to a sudden threat, and he is in an alarm response. At the moment it's not a bad sign; it's a very good sign, in fact. A sign that all battle stations are ready. The hands, the feet, and the stomach—they're all sacrificing for the cause.

The thickness of Ugh's blood changes, too. Blood platelets are sent to the blood stream to thicken the blood in case the tiger bites him. Thick blood clots faster and makes it harder to bleed to death. Other changes occur simultaneously. Ugh's hearing becomes more acute (the better to hear the tiger) and his eyes dilate (the better to see the tiger). Everything he needs to physically survive—to fight or to flee—is put in place because his life is on the line, and these are the natural physiological responses.

So that's the alarm response, and in this case, and for Ugh's sake, let's say it worked. Ugh sees the tiger in time and uses his sudden burst of energy to smack the tiger with his club, and then he runs back to his cave, where he rolls a huge rock over the opening. Safe to live another day!

THE ALARM RESPONSE

Now it's the next day, and while searching for food to satisfy his need to live, Ugh is walking down the same path where he encountered the tiger the day before.

What's Ugh saying to himself? It's not hard to imagine him repeating to himself, "Where's the tiger!" "Where's the tiger!" Ugh is going to be anything but nonchalant and casual. He's ready. Any movement in the brush, he's there. Any little thing, he's prepared. He's in what is called a vigilant state, and his body is already into a viligant response.

There's a difference between the alarm response Ugh had yesterday and the vigilant response he's now experiencing. The alarm response called for action; the vigilant response calls for preparation, in case action is needed. As Ugh walks down the path, he is heavy into preparation.

To prepare for another possible tiger encounter, the adrenal gland doesn't produce adrenaline as it would for an actual attack, but instead releases a hormone called cortisol. Like its cousin adrenaline, cortisol triggers a number of chemical reactions in Ugh's body, some of them similar to those caused by adrenaline and some not so similar.

Cortisol is the hormone of preparation. One of the things it can do is trigger the liver to increase its production of cholesterol. While cholesterol is looked at mainly today as a menace to society, it definitely has its beneficial purposes, primarily as a repair agent. The same stickiness property that causes cholesterol to clog arteries also allows it to line and repair cells—a most useful property in Ugh's body, if he's going to have to battle that tiger again today. He's bound to damage some cells, and extra cholesterol is already in store to help him if that happens. Another useful purpose of cholesterol is to lubricate and pad the joints, something Ugh will also need in the event of an encounter with the tiger.

It's also educational to note that the two forms of cholesterol (HDL = good cholesterol, LDL = bad cholesterol) also relate to Ugh.

Survival responses trigger the sticky bad cholesterol (LDL) to repair cells. And what's the biggest factor in raising good cholesterol (HDL), which binds to carry away the bad cholesterol? You guessed it, physical exertion—exactly what Ugh does when he fights or runs from the tiger.

Cortisol also triggers the body to retain fluids. If Ugh is going to fight or flee he'll need to sweat more so that his body temperature will remain cool, and cortisol helps take care of that. Similarly, body fat stores go up, and Ugh, in this preparation stage, will have a craving for sugars and fats. If it's fight or flight, those sources of fuel will need to be on hand. Also, cortisol triggers Ugh's immune system to shut down. Now you may ask yourself, why on earth would his immune system shut down? The answer is that it's his immune system that constantly requires the most energy, and at the moment Ugh doesn't need his immune system nearly as much as he needs all available energy to either fight harder or run faster. He isn't worried about getting sick, not at this moment, he's worried about living. So the immune system shuts down, temporarily, so the energy it usually uses can become a part of the survival response. If the tiger comes around the bend, Ugh is as ready as he'll ever be.

The Cost Is Toxic

There is a price to pay for all this preparedness, however, and that price is in the form of toxins, or poisons. Every time the body has a chemical reaction there is a byproduct, or a toxin, that's released. Just as in a nuclear reaction there is radioactivity or fallout, in the same manner, whenever your body triggers chemical reactions there's a toxin that is released as a result. To facilitate his primitive survival responses, either alarm or vigilance, Ugh would have up to 1,400 chemical reactions—and he would have a fairly equivalent amount of resultant toxins released into his bloodstream. When Ugh fights or runs, these toxins are no problem—they're either burned up or sweated out of the body. During the first twelve minutes of physical exertion the body burns exclusively what's in the blood stream. So when Ugh physically exerts he's burning toxins. As he sweats, he purges more toxins. Thus Ugh dissipates the poison. He gets rid of the toxic byproducts of adrenaline and cortisol.

Now I'm going to deliver some good news and bad news as we bring the example of Ugh into the present day.

The good news is that the same adrenaline and cortisol reactions experienced by Ugh are still available today. Like stone-age Ugh, each of us has the Incredible Hulk inside. Have you ever read about a woman lifting a car to save a child? How did she do it? Adrenaline! That power has not been lost over the centuries. We still use adrenaline and cortisol on a regular basis.

The bad news is that when we get upset over a soda machine swallowing our dollar bill, our blood thickens in case the soda machine bites us.

INTRODUCING DOUG

Look at the picture of Doug, the modern-day Ugh (see illustration). Just as Ugh fought the saber-toothed tiger, Doug fights the soda machine. Whereas Ugh's battles centered around physical threats, Doug's center mostly around mental threats.

Doug wants a soda. He puts in his money. But this machine hasn't come through for Doug before, and he's not entirely sure what to expect. As he pushes the button for the soda of his choice he's already braced for a confrontation—a confrontation with an inanimate machine!

At this point, Doug's body is responding exactly as Ugh's body responded when Ugh came down the path wondering if the tiger was going to be there. It's going into a vigilant response. The adrenal gland is producing cortisol, the liver is increasing its production of cholesterol, the cortisol is ordering the body to retain fluids and to shut down its immune system, and all of the resultant chemical reactions are releasing thousands of toxins into his system. Toxins that ultimately will have nowhere to go. Why will they have nowhere to go? Because Doug's fight with the soda machine is mental. The machine can not hurt him physically.

For the most part, our modern lives revolve around mental obstacles and threats, not physical obstacles and threats. Not many of our threats have a lot to do with physical survival anymore; they're not driven by the need to live. We don't run into many saber-toothed tigers. But the body doesn't know the difference.

Whether the perceived threat is mental or physical, the body will respond with adrenaline and cortisol. Anytime there is the perception of a threat (remember, that's our definition of stress) our cholesterol is going to go up, we'll retain fats and sugars, our immune systems will shut down, our digestion will become acidic, and toxins will flood the body. But today, whenever we have a mental threat, what do we do with the toxins? Do we fight or flee? The answer is, Almost never. We may mentally exert, but we rarely physically exert. The result? Too often we are left literally to stew in our juices.

If you've ever cooked stew, have you noticed how the meat in the stew deteriorates and falls apart as the juices around it break it down? Well, these mental threats cause what I call "heart stew." When toxins are allowed to go unchecked in the body, the same thing happens to our hearts that happens to the meat in stew. Left to accumulate in the heart muscle tissue, toxins will break down the heart muscle and form what's called a contraction band lesion. The contraction band is that band of muscle that makes your heart contract. When toxins are left lingering in the heart muscle a lesion develops, and the heart is seriously weakened.

SILENT KILLERS

Contraction band lesions are by no means the only complications of modern-day mental threats, but they are representative of the many forms of silent killers that are at work in our modern society. Statistics indicate that contraction band lesions are found in 86 percent of the approximately 400,000 sudden deaths annually reported in the United States. This isn't a minor symptom. This is no small problem. Its prevalence is staggering. Probably the most disturbing part is that our modern-day heart testing systems aren't designed to detect the problem. They're set up to test us physically, not mentally.

Think about it. How do doctors test us today to see how we're responding physically to our mental threats? They'll put us on a treadmill or a heart-rate monitor, or they'll measure our EKG and our oxygen intake capacity or test our blood pressure. Let's say you go in and get your blood pressure tested, and the doctor says, "Your blood pressure's great, get out of here." That afternoon you die of a heart attack. Why didn't the doctor pick it up? Maybe it's because you like your doctor; you're relaxed in his or her office, and you think your doctor's a great doctor. So your doctor is not something you consider to be an obstacle or a threat, and your blood pressure is fine in the office. It's a chance for you to relax from the pressures of your busy schedule.

The point is, it isn't easy to physically test to see if we're building toxins to a dangerous level in our bodies. The only way I could accurately test your blood pressure as it relates to anxiety and stress is if I hooked you up to a blood pressure cuff for twenty-four hours around the clock and profiled what your blood pressure did all day long. Different situations trigger different results as do different times of the year. There have been studies, for example, that show a CPA's cholesterol level going up by as much as 100 points during tax season and then going back down again when the returns have all been mailed off to the IRS.

It's important to know if we're accumulating toxins. If we're constantly going into a vigilant response and rarely, if ever, entering the action-response phase, that's plain unhealthy! We're the human equivalent of a fireplace with the chimney closed.

Bear in mind that we are not talking about doing away with adrenaline and cortisol. To the contrary. Those two natural hormones are valuable in our lives. In some of our occupations and recreational pursuits, it's imperative that they are present to help us perform better.

Know What's Going On

We need to better control how and when to release adrenaline and cortisol. It's important to know what's going on with the adrenaline and cortisol we have at our disposal so we can use them effectively and take care to rid ourselves of the resultant toxins. If we are constantly triggering adrenaline and cortisol in reaction to mental obstacles only and we aren't physically exerting to reduce the buildup of toxicity, then we're in trouble (whether we know it or not), and we need to do something about it.

That doesn't mean that if the boss gets my blood pressure up first thing in the morning that I go to the boss and say, "Boss, you're stressing me out and I've got toxins, so I've got to go physically exert. I've got to release them. I'll be back in a minute." The procedure doesn't have to be that immediate. It's like with a tooth. If you eat food and leave it unchecked in your teeth for twenty-four hours it turns to plaque and starts the decaying process. Does that mean you'll have a cavity the next day or the day after that? No. It takes a while to decay a tooth. It's the same way with the heart muscle. It won't decay overnight. If we go three or four days building up toxins and don't physically exert, that doesn't necessarily mean we're going to get a contraction band lesion. But we're going to be in trouble if we let it go unchecked indefinitely. If we're aware of the possible toxicity levels going on inside our bodies and have some kind of consistent physical exertion to counteract that, we can do like Ugh and get rid of the poisons. We can avoid the deadly combination of a pressurized workload and no physical exertion.

BIOPSY OR AUTOPSY

I get asked a lot if it's possible to detect a contraction band lesion. I say yes, there are two ways: with a biopsy or an autopsy! The next question I get asked is if it's possible to get rid of, or repair, a contraction band lesion that already exists. The answer, unfortunately, is no. Whenever we damage muscle tissue we form scar tissue, and we cannot get rid of scar tissue. That doesn't mean we're left without remedies. Through exercise, we can build healthy tissue around the scar tissue already formed. We can always strengthen that which has been weakened, even if we can't go back and start over.

As we leave Ugh and Doug we find that we're basically left with two choices. Either we do away with adrenaline and cortisol, or we physically exert to eliminate the harmful toxins and the potentially dangerous physical conditions, such as contraction band lesions, that adrenaline and cortisol are capable of producing. Those are our choices, and it should be obvious which choice is in our best interest.

For those of us who have jobs that adrenaline helps us perform better, an exercise schedule is critical. The same thing that was true for Ugh's body is true for our bodies: We were made to move. We're meant to physically exert.

We can literally save our lives by understanding what's going on inside of us—and doing something about it—as we deal with modern-day mental obstacles that we perceive as threats. We can see modern-day saber-toothed tigers all around us in our workplaces today. The soda machine is not alone as a potential stressor.

Awareness is the key to the cure, just as awareness is the key to recognizing that, unlike saber-toothed tigers, our modern-day obstacles and threats are in large measure defined by us. We're luckier than Ugh. The saber-toothed tiger was a saber-toothed tiger with real saber teeth no matter what he thought. He couldn't wish it away. He couldn't get rid of the problem by changing his perception. But we *can* wish many of our threats away. In our modern mental experiences, we can create saber-toothed tigers or we can eliminate saber-toothed tigers. They can come with or without teeth—all according to our perceptions, which are a result of our beliefs. When we put correct beliefs in place, the result will be an elimination of many of our "tigers."

Instant Replay

Key Points

- Diseases of stress are diseases of choice.

- We can't always control what happens to us, but we can control what happens inside us.

- Stress is how we respond to events based upon our perception.

- Our bodies are meant to move. That's how we release toxins. Good health depends on it.

Personal Exercise

Take an inventory of the times you missed work or took prescription drugs during the past year. Was the root cause a contagious disease or a disease of choice?

Where Do We Go from Here?

In chapter six, we'll look at warning lights that, if heeded, can prevent diseases of choice and, if ignored, can lead to addictions that cater to these diseases.

Don't Sacrifice What You Want Most for What You Want Now

Take it from an old distance runner—it's the long run that matters.

As a runner I've developed a keen appreciation for endurance. I admire stamina and a strong will. Probably that's why one of my favorite characters in literature is the old fisherman in Ernest Hemingway's classic book *The Old Man and the Sea.* Hemingway doesn't tell us much background about the old man, only that his name is Santiago, and he's a fisherman who's spent his days working the waters off the Cuban coastline. We get to know the old man well as he hooks a giant fish, a catch of a lifetime, and holds on as days turn into nights and back into days again. It's really too much for the old man, this ordeal, but he won't cut the line because all his life he's been in search of a great fish like this. Whenever the pain and the fatigue seem to be unbearable, the old man has some terrific talks with himself that are the real essence of the book:

> It was a great temptation to rest in the bow and let the fish make one circle by himself without recovering any line. But when the strain showed the fish had turned to come toward the boat, the old man rose to his feet and started the pivoting and the weaving pulling that brought in all the line he gained.
>
> I'm tireder than I have ever been, he thought, and now the

trade wind is rising. But that will be good to take him in with. I need that badly.

He does not let go. The old man knew what he wanted and refused to give up so he could be more comfortable for the moment. Talk about self-help! No one else was there to do it for him, so he talked himself into it.

THINK LONG-TERM

It may be an extreme example and one that's far from the waters we might fish in, but it has some definite parallels to the concept of belief-driven behavior and the forces of fatigue that try to short-circuit our attempts to achieve our personal best. The old man's beliefs were firmly in place, and he wasn't about to deviate from them. What he wanted most was to be a great fisherman, and landing this great fish would validate that; it was a course he would not turn from, even if it meant being dragged bleeding and broken halfway to Venezuela. He would not sacrifice what he wanted most for what he wanted now.

That's a Natural Law we would all do well to commit to memory:

Don't sacrifice what you want most for what you want now.

Just as the old man knew that by hanging on to the fish, he would, over the long haul, satisfy his need (in this case primarily his self-worth need), if we know what our goals are then we can satisfy our various needs by hanging on to those things that are true to our beliefs. The old man's life may have been simpler than ours, it's true, and we may have conflicts he could never have dreamed of out there alone on the high seas. But the similarities are still there. If we understand the need to establish beliefs that are correct for us and then behave in a manner that's consistent with those beliefs no matter what, we can satisfy our needs and truly get what we want most, just like the old man.

But if we choose to consistently act in a manner that will allow us to satisfy our four needs right now (and remember, satisfying those needs is a daily process), we will always be inclined to take the path of least resistance.

THE PATH OF LEAST PAIN

The path of least resistance is the path that looks inviting and promising. It's the path of least pain, and that's compelling. It's the easiest way to go. For the old man it meant letting go of the fish so he could rest. For us, it means letting go of hopes and dreams so we can feel good right now.

But it's a path that goes in circles, a path that gets us nowhere. And too often it's a path that leads us to addictions that ensure we will remain in that circle.

By our definition, an addiction is habitual behavior that produces short-term satisfaction and long-term harm. The reason we have addictions in our lives is because we want to satisfy our four needs now. Not over time, today.

Addictions are a short-term way of dealing with the threats and symptoms we talked about in the last chapter. They help us deal with the obstacles immediately. Not later, now. Addictions fix things right now. But the problem is, it's only temporary.

ADDICTIONS IN THEIR MANY FORMS

Take a minute and you can think of any number of addictions. Medications are a good example. We've already discussed what a booming business the pain medication business is in this country, and in most cases these medications do nothing to cure what's wrong. Their purpose is to treat the symptoms. When we have a headache and take an aspirin, for instance, we don't really get rid of the root cause of the headache. All the aspirin does is mask the pain so we don't feel it until the reason causing the headache goes away. But the pain is still there. If we never do anything about the obstacle (the problem) that's causing the headache (the symptom) in the first place, the headache will keep returning, and we'll keep going to the medicine cabinet for aspirin. The circle will spin and spin and spin.

Sleeping is a popular, if less visible, addiction. That's one way to keep the obstacles and threats away for a while. Just sleep it off. But are the obstacles and threats gone when we finally decide to wake up?

Avoidance can be another addiction, as well as denial, procrastination, blame, working overtime, and any of thousands of other "masks." Consider each of these potential addictions one by one. All are excellent at masking and delaying pain and keeping our lives stagnant.

Shopping can be an addiction when it's used for the purpose of a short-term satisfaction that masks whatever it is that has the potential of causing us long-term harm. Not only that, it can cost us a lot of money.

How about watching television as an addiction? Americans watch, on the average, thirty-three hours of TV a week. Why? It's one of the least painful things a person can do—sit and be entertained with your beverage of choice in one hand and a bowl of chips in the other. What's hard about that?

What can watching that much television get in the way of? Relationships that need work, occupational duties, exercise, making new friends, and the list goes on and on.

Virtually anything can be an addiction if we choose to use it as such. Work can even be an addiction, or family, if we use it to excess as a way of avoiding or delaying things that are important to us.

THE TWIN BIG ONES

Two of the most obvious addictions in our modern society are, of course, alcohol and tobacco. By addictions I'm not referring to, or entering the debate about, the well-known addictiveness of alcohol and nicotine. In the context of principle-driven behavior, I'm talking about the potential alcohol and tobacco have for allowing us to mask and avoid.

Statistics show that the abuse of these products is enormous. According to research by the National Public Services Research Institute, a nonprofit policy research organization located in Washington, D.C., the cost in dollars alone is astronomical.

In a recent news article, Ted Miller, the associate director of the Institute, reported the following:

- Alcohol-related costs to the American society, including medical spending, lost wages, and lost hours of work, total $128 billion a year—the equivalent of fifty cents per drink consumed annually.

  Direct cost to the nation for alcohol-related automobile accidents is $44 billion yearly.

- Tobacco rings up a health-care bill of $94.4 billion every year, according to the Center on Addiction and Substance Abuse at Columbia University in New York. Eighty percent of all substance-abuse costs, the center estimates, are related to tobacco.

These aren't statistics that show what Americans are paying merely to purchase and use alcohol and tobacco, they're statistics to show what Americans are paying *because* of the use of these popular addictions. These costs are just damage control.

NOBODY WINS THE ADDICTION GAME

The key to understanding addiction is to recognize that it's the culprit that causes us to sacrifice what we want most for what we want now. If we sacrifice what we want most it will throw us into a vigilant response mode. Because of that we'll get the cortisol flowing because what's happening is unsettling. As time goes on it will typically grind at us more and more; it will compound and build and agitate. We'll stay in a constant state of anxiety, always preparing for battle (and never going). We'll gear up and get upset and uptight. Then we'll never actually physically battle anything. All that cortisol at work won't do us any good. To the contrary, it will do us a lot of harm if we don't physically exert and rid ourselves of the toxins.

That's just one of the downsides of addictions. They prevent us from dealing with what's hurting us. Most of the time they prevent us from even realizing what it is. The reason why we don't confront the real source of the pain is because we've become slaves to our addictions, whatever ones we might have chosen, and those addictions don't allow us to change our behavior. They mask the pain and call off the fight. They don't allow us to get what we want most. We're always too busy paying attention to and taking care of the now.

Addictions usually start out innocently enough. I like to refer to them in the beginning as Band-Aids. Band-Aids aren't bad in and of themselves. But the problem with Band-Aids is they can become addictions over time. Band-Aids cover up our problems so we don't have to deal with them. If we're not careful, they will completely cover up the signals that tell us there's a problem that needs our attention.

BAND-AIDS DON'T SOLVE ANYTHING

Think of the warning lights in your car. If you're driving down the street and the "check engine" light comes on, what should you do? Pull over and stop, of course. But do we do that? I know of a person who saw the "check engine" light go on in his car and responded by actually putting a Band-Aid over the light so it wouldn't be annoying. This was a very busy person who couldn't be bothered by that red light, so he reached into the first-aid kit in his glove compartment and took care of the red light. Well, not long after that his engine burned up. It was drained completely of oil. When the towing company hauled the car to the service department the mechanics looked inside and there was the Band-Aid, right where it had been left.

We have warning lights go on in our body all the time. In many cases they are symptoms before they become addictions. If we start to sleep too much, for example, that's probably a warning light that a problem needs to be looked at and dealt with. But too often we'll ignore that warning signal and simply continue to oversleep. As we continue to oversleep we'll become addicted to that short-term fix. We'll ignore "sleeping" as a warning light and turn it into an addiction—something that helps us mask the pain and feel better now.

In our complex lives we need to be more aware than ever of what's weighing on our minds. It's only when we get in tune with our warning lights that we put ourselves in a position to do something about what turned them on.

WARNING LIGHTS COME IN THREE CONVENIENT FORMS

We also should be aware that warning lights generally come on in three different ways. We can see a warning light through a physical response, such as the "check engine" light in the car. Physical-response warning lights are the easiest to recognize, understand, and respond to. They are the pains—headaches, stomachaches, tension, chest pains—that tell us something's wrong, and we ought to do something about it. Although they are the easiest to recognize, they can also be the most deadly when ignored.

The second way warning lights come on is through emotional responses, such as the desire to oversleep or a chronic habit of denial. Emotional-response warning lights are generally more subtle. They're the ones that require us to be in tune with the beliefs on our belief windows and the behavior those beliefs drive. Emotional warning lights come in the form of depression, anxiety, fear, frustration, and anger. They need to be listened to, not ignored.

The third area of warning lights is the one I consider the most important. If you'll recall the Reality Model you'll remember that we labeled the "mental response" as our trigger. Our mental responses, or self-talks, are the triggers for our behavior. These warning lights are mental responses mostly in the form of self-talks, like the old fisherman had with himself as he went through the ordeal of landing his big fish. Self-talks are the conversations we have with ourselves.

DON'T TALK—OR TALK BACK—NEGATIVELY

Very often the reason things cause us distress is because of the negative self-talks we've had about them. We develop negative self-talks because we have a perception of a threat (we're "stressed"), and we conclude we better battle that threat. Thus, a vicious cycle can begin. Surveys have shown that up to 80 percent of our self-talks are negative. If we have negative self-talks going on all the time then what are we triggering all the time? We're triggering the emotional and physical survival responses as evidenced by the symptoms we've discussed. Then we start to use Band-Aids to cover the symptoms, which, when left unnoticed, can lead to addictions.

Consider the boss as a source of distress. Why do bosses stress people out? The most common response is because the boss doesn't respect me. The boss doesn't check with me, the boss doesn't ask for my opinion, the boss doesn't tell me "nice job," and a whole lot of other things that can indicate a lack of respect and create dissatisfaction with the boss.

Now, what happens every time we run the above negative self-talk tapes about bosses in our minds? We reinforce our belief. Every time we see the boss, every time we think about the boss, those are the kind of tapes we run.

We can change our tapes. We have the power to do that. We can create new self-talks that trigger different responses. We can turn the 80 percent negative self-talks into 80 percent positive self-talks, and more. We can recognize the warning lights that come from negative self-talks and eliminate addictions, if we use our self-talks as warning lights and not as negative reinforcement.

Self-Talks Keep Us in Touch with Beliefs

What will our self-talks get us in touch with? They'll get us in touch with our beliefs, of course. When we perceive the boss as a threat because he doesn't respect us, we're behaving according to a belief we have that says something along the lines of "My self-worth is tied to what the boss thinks of me." Since my perception is that the boss doesn't respect me, where does that leave my self-worth? But if in our self-talk we decide to change our belief to "My self-worth is tied to how well I do my job, regardless of whether the boss notices," we will satisfy our self-worth need *and* eliminate the pitfall of addiction.

How about a self-talk regarding this belief: "Being successful brings more responsibility and more work for us to handle." Since we already have more than enough to do, what does that belief inherently imply? We'll try not to be very successful, of course. We'll behave in such a way that makes us appear unsuccessful—or at least as unsuccessful as possible and still keep our jobs. We'll not be gracious at accepting praise, we'll procrastinate getting our work finished; we'll complain about our workload, be difficult to work with, and try to shift our work onto our coworkers. All this because of our belief that says "Being successful makes more work."

It's easy to imagine that the results of our behavior will be frustration, cynicism, and probably also exhaustion, since it requires a lot of energy to get out of work. We also won't be very popular with our coworkers and our bosses (especially when it comes to raises and promotions).

Since these results hardly qualify as satisfying our needs—in this case our self-worth and need to live—our self-talks would need to reflect that. We would say to ourselves, "What if I looked at being successful in another way? What if I looked at all the positives that come from being successful? People praise me when I'm successful. People like me when I'm successful. I have an opportunity to help the company grow and become more productive when I'm successful. I have an opportunity to help others when I'm successful." With that kind of self-talk in mind, we're then in a position to change our belief to "Being successful gives me the freedom to move on and be myself."

Self-talk is the trigger that drives new beliefs onto our belief windows, enabling us to behave in a manner quite different from our old behavior. Again, this doesn't mean we have to sacrifice our other needs. Our self-talks can also include self-instruction that says we don't have to accept promotions that are the result of our success, if those promotions mean spending more time at work and less time fulfilling our need for love at home or our need for variety at the golf course. That's the beauty of self-talks. They're ours and ours alone. We can talk ourselves into seeing things the way we want to see them for healthy outlooks.

WHEN YOU TALK YOU USUALLY LISTEN

There's the story about the guy in the circus whose job was to follow the elephants and camels and horses on the parade into town and clean up any droppings they happened to leave on the pavement. Somebody watching the parade at the side of the road yells out, "How can you lower yourself like that? How can you perform such a despicable task? Why don't you quit?" To which the circus guy says, "What, and give up show business?"

That's obviously a person who's had some long and effective self-talks.

The world is full of examples of people who use the power of self-talks. We could also call them self-motivators. They are our own internal "halftime speeches." They inspire us to keep a positive attitude, reminding us that we can succeed.

Can you imagine the self-talks Charles Lindbergh must have had as he crossed the Atlantic alone in his airplane? No one else was there to motivate him, to keep him awake and focused. He had to rely on himself. Self-talks are especially important at those moments when we have to decide whether to continue on or abandon ship.

Self-talks can come in many forms. Some people cover their bathroom mirror with slogans, poems, sayings, and other reminders of their goals and beliefs. Others memorize these same slogans, poems, and sayings. In whatever form, their purpose is the same—to keep us in touch with what we want most. They keep us focused. A few seasons ago, Karl Malone, a basketball player for the Utah Jazz, started chanting to himself just prior to shooting free throws. Although he was accomplished in virtually all other areas of the game, Malone had some difficulty with his free throw percentage, so he turned to self-talks to increase his effectiveness. When asked what he said to himself, he politely declined to reveal the content of those conversations. They were private, he said.

SELF-TALKS PREVENT OVERSTATING OUR TROUBLES

If our self-talks are positive they'll allow us to look at our lives in ways that are best for us. They'll help us put things in perspective. They'll help us stop short of catastrophizing—of using big labels for little things. How often in our negative self-talks do we say something is horrible? Well, what's horrible? The famines in Africa. The Holocaust. Right? But is it horrible if I'm late for work? Is it horrible if my coworker didn't finish his or her work and left it on my desk? Our self-talks should help us to either use appropriate labels or not label at all. They can have a tremendous impact. I remember walking past a graveyard in Florida and seeing a tombstone with this epitaph: "I Told You I Was Sick." If that's the kind of self-talks the deceased engaged in, maybe he quickened the process.

Our self-talks ought to be positive. They should allow us to see life with hope and enthusiasm, not with dread and foreboding. Hope can spring eternal, when it's internal.

It all ties together when we think about it. To paraphrase Benjamin Franklin: We can't always control what goes on around us, but we can control what goes on inside us.

Instant Replay

Key Points

- The path of least resistance is the path of least pain.

- Addictions satisfy our needs now!

- Our body's warning lights come in three forms—physical, emotional, and mental (self-talks).

- Self-talks are the most important warning light because they trigger our behavior.

Personal Exercise

Make a list of your warning lights. Have they become an addiction?

Where Do We Go from Here?

In chapter seven, we'll look at the preventive medicine we all can practice to build ourselves mentally, emotionally, and physically.

CHAPTER SEVEN

Exercise Only on the Days That You Eat

Preventive medicine wards off afflictions and effectively deals with the hurdles that get in our way. You can't do more with your life than you are physically, mentally, and emotionally capable of doing.

Now that we've become more aware of the obstacles and threats that are bound to come our way, let's discuss some ways to effectively respond to life's challenges. First, it's important to remember that our responses will come in one of three areas: We'll have physical, mental, or emotional responses and often a blend of all three. An understanding of the peculiarities of each area is important in outlining an effective principle-based game plan.

Accepting the fact that some obstacles and threats are a necessary fact of life, no matter what we do, it follows that it's important to plan in advance those ways to best deal with them. Are there practical, sensible things we can do to make the process easier, to prepare ourselves before the threat comes in and knocks us over? Are there strategies we can put in place that will actually make the journey enjoyable? Are there ways to satisfy our correct principles in spite of the threats? The answer is a resounding Yes!

Remember these six words: *A healthy lifestyle is preventive medicine.* Or, if you prefer to turn those six words around: *Preventive medicine is a healthy lifestyle.*

ANTIDOTE TO ADDICTIONS

Preventive medicine refers to those things we can do to prepare for whatever obstacles might come our way. It is the antidote to addictions: preparation that will enable us to absorb the challenges represented by those obstacles; preparation that allows us to handle the obstacles instead of them handling us. In many cases, we can actually use the obstacles to make us stronger, to help us grow.

To begin with, I think it's important to appreciate the simple reality that we can only accomplish with our lives what we physically, mentally, and emotionally prepare ourselves to accomplish. We can't go beyond our own preparation and endurance. We can't use magic and mirrors.

It's been said that we can't do more than we are physically capable of doing. Likewise we can't do more than we are emotionally and mentally capable of doing. Hence our mental, emotional, and physical strength is going to determine the limits of our activities and achievements. None of us are superhuman. We have our limits. But it's preparation that helps us stretch our capabilities to their fullest extent. With preparation, we put ourselves in position to be the best that we can be.

Let me use this situation to illustrate: If I had two hours of sleep last night will I respond to the exact same threat differently than if I had eight hours of sleep? Of course I'll respond differently. How much sleep I have will determine how well I can take things on. It will determine how much energy I'll have. If I had two hours of sleep I'll likely respond irritably and impatiently. If I had eight hours of sleep I'll likely respond more positively.

Sleep serves as just one simple example of how we can implement a "preventive behavior" that will qualify as preventive medicine. Getting the amount of sleep that's right for us will make us more resilient when it comes to dealing with life's events. By making sure we're well rested, we've reduced our susceptibility to obstacles. We're stronger, more energetic, more patient; we're better able to cope. We're better *prepared*. When we understand that, then we realize the importance of using sleep as a way to best prepare for the next day, not as just something we do when we're exhausted.

FIVE GENERAL CATEGORIES

In general, preventive behaviors tend to fit into one of five categories. These include the areas of fitness and nutrition, finances, relationships, mental and emotional stability, and creativity and expression. Each of these areas greatly impacts our physical, mental, or emotional responses. There are a variety of things we can do not only to avoid the obstacles lurking in each of these areas, but to turn them into positives that will in turn bring us inner peace and real harmony as they are fused with the beliefs on our belief windows.

FITNESS AND NUTRITION

You and I and just about everyone in the twentieth century knows that the hardest part about exercising is getting started. Since we now know about the toxins left in our body because of survival responses, don't we have even more reason to get started? Knowledge can be a wonderful motivator. I would suggest keeping the following list handy, for motivational purposes. Apply these "Ten Tips" in your life, and if it isn't already, exercise can become a regular, and even enjoyable, part of your lifestyle.

1. Give aerobic exercise an "A" priority a minimum of every other day.
2. Identify a variety of aerobic exercises you enjoy. Select two or three different ones to do on a regular basis.
3. Look for a variety of enjoyable places to do your aerobic exercise. Be sure to include alternatives for stormy weather.
4. Choose your best time of day to exercise and be consistent. Remember to wait a minimum of one hour after you eat.

(Or, better yet, exercise before you eat and surprise yourself at how much your appetite will be suppressed.)

5. Start out slow. Always finish an exercise session feeling like you could have done more, not like you wish you'd never started.

6. Work out to music when possible. Research shows that music actually raises exercise tolerance levels and makes a workout seem easier (which goes a long way in explaining how Rocky always managed to get in shape so fast). Keep the volume on headphones at a low level if you're exercising outside, however, so you can hear what's around you (such as big trucks and mad dogs).

7. Work out with a friend or join groups; surround yourself with people who share similar exercise goals.

8. Play at your progress. Do what you did last week a little faster or stronger this week, just a little. Change your courses and challenges regularly for variety.

9. Reward yourself. Every time you work out, for example, pay yourself a dollar, or five dollars. It's your money. Put the money in a special fund for something you really want, like new running shoes.

10. Take an energy inventory. Compare your energy level on the days you work out with the days you don't work out. You may find you're soon working out virtually every day, because you realize how much better it makes you feel.

Do It for Health

Of course the best tip of all is to exercise because you *want to*. For a lot of people—probably a majority of people—that's easier said than realized. For a lot of people exercise is work, plain and simple; a necessary evil, maybe. But why should we want to exercise? So we can get what we want most, that's why. Exercise is the most effective way to avoid the contraction band lesions we talked about in chapter four.

It's the most effective way to lower blood pressure. It's the most effective way to have healthy hearts. The benefits are legend. How can we get what we want most if we don't have our physical health? Remember the results of the University of North Carolina study in chapter two, where the four thousand retired executives lamented "throwing away my health as if it were trash." With the proper use of self-talks, it's possible actually to want to exercise.

Let's talk about blood pressure and heart disease, two of the most prevalent health threats of the twentieth century. The best way to lower blood pressure and reduce the risk of heart disease is to strengthen the heart muscle. Build it up. Make it so strong that when your doctor listens to it he gets a huge smile on his face. The stronger your heart, the more blood it's capable of pumping with each stroke. The more blood the heart is capable of pumping with each stroke, the lower your blood pressure and the lower your resting heart rate. For strong hearts, the tugs and pulls of everyday life become a piece of cake, so to speak. It's easy to get a good read on just how strong your heart is by measuring your resting pulse rate. When you're stationary and relaxed, look at your watch or a clock and put your index finger on a major blood vessel such as the jugular vein in your neck. Count the number of beats for ten seconds. Then multiply by six to get the number of times your heart beats per minute. Between seventy and eighty beats per minute is considered normal. Anything over that indicates a heart that needs strengthening. Anything under seventy indicates a stronger than average heart. Below sixty is getting stronger. Below fifty is better yet. Below forty and you might consider entering the next Boston Marathon or Tour de France.

Bear in mind that aerobic exercise is anything we do that raises our heartbeat to our target heart rate for at least twenty minutes. Whenever we engage in aerobic exercise we work out our heart muscle. When I was in college I got a very vivid education as to the results of aerobic exercise when they gave echocardiograms to the track team. We had a big guy from Sweden on our team who threw the shot put, and he and I went for our echocardiograms at the same time. When

121

our tests were done they took the pictures they'd taken of our hearts and backlit them so we could see what they looked like. The shot putter was about twice as big as me, with these huge muscles all over his body that were twice as big as mine. But my heart muscle was twice as big as his. Why? I like to think it's because I'm all heart. What those echocardiograms really showed was that I regularly worked out aerobically, and he did not.

The shot putter worked out with huge weights that built up his biceps, his triceps, his quads, and his deltoids. I worked out by running long distances, and that mostly built up my heart. The muscles we worked all the time were big and strong; the ones we paid little attention to weren't so big and strong. It's that simple. In the long run, the heart muscle is the most important. It won't get you many stares on the beach, but it will keep you going to the beach for a long, long time.

Mix It Up

Of course, modern physiologists have found that a mixture of aerobic exercise with weight lifting can be a most effective combination. Working with weights develops lean muscle mass, and the body will respond with a higher metabolic rate anytime it has additional muscle mass to support. Aerobic exercise mixed with weight work gives the body a kind of double signal to increase its metabolism.

The beauty of aerobic exercise is that it doesn't have to be overly time-consuming for maximum results. Thirty minutes a day at your target heart rate will maintain a high level of fitness. If you want to train for a marathon or a century bike race, or if you want to swim the English Channel or climb Mount Everest, fine. That may be the best kind of motivation to keep your interest level high. But it isn't necessary. All the body asks is consistent maintenance. You don't even need to exercise every day. *Exercise only on the days that you eat.* Give it thirty minutes every day, and the rewards can be tremendous. Give it more than that, and the results will build even more.

Aerobic exercise also goes well beyond working out the heart muscle. Done regularly, it also:

- reduces levels of so-called bad cholesterol (Low-Density Lipoproteins) and increases levels of good cholesterol (High-Density Lipoproteins);

- changes your food cravings from fats and sugars to the fuel foods, or carbohydrates;

- raises your metabolic rate.

The last two are especially significant because they apply positively to nutrition and weight loss—two very common concerns in our modern lives. Indeed, the preoccuption with being overweight is not just one of the biggest concerns in our modern society but also one of our biggest stressors. It demands a great deal of time, attention, and concern that could otherwise be placed elsewhere.

Starvation Isn't Worth It

The whole key to how much fat your body carries is your metabolic rate, or the base rate at which your body burns calories. It follows, then, that the key to weight loss is raising metabolic rate. The higher the rate, the more fat you burn. Now think about this for a minute. If you go on a starvation diet what do you do to your metabolic rate? You slow it down. What kind of foods does your body crave? Right, sugars and fats. The reason it craves the high-calorie sugars and fats is because they can be stored and later used as fuel. When you're starving yourself, your body instinctively goes into a survival mode to protect you from starvation. It doesn't know the difference between a diet and a famine. When no food is coming in it intuitively lowers its metabolic rate and sends out alarm signals for sugars and fats. That's why restrictive calorie diets don't work. Sooner or later the body will take over and go on a sugar and fat binge, piling all the weight back on. Studies have shown that 90 percent of people who go on a starvation diet actually weigh *more* a year later.

If this information stops you from ever going on a restrictive calorie diet, that's great. Take the information a step further. If metabolic rate determines how much fat your body burns, then what will be the only truly effective diet? Anything that raises your metabolic rate is the answer. What raises your metabolic rate? Exercise, that's what. Just as your body will overcompensate in the face of a starvation diet—shutting down beyond where it needs to—it will overcompensate in the other direction when you exercise.

Not only will you burn more calories because you're exercising, but by raising your base metabolic rate that means you'll burn more calories all the time. You'll burn them at a higher rate when you're resting, even when you're sleeping. After an aerobic exercise your body doesn't immediately lower the metabolic rate. You experience what's known as a post-workout burn, and your metabolic rate will only come down gradually over a forty-eight-hour period. If you exercise again within that forty-eight-hour period you never go back to the metabolic rate you were at before you started exercising. Pretty soon you've raised your bottom level, and if you keep exercising it keeps going up, at least to a point. This is why people at their ideal weight eat more than people who are overweight and still don't gain weight.

If you try to lose weight permanently without exercising you might as well beat your head against the wall, because your body doesn't know how to do it. You're essentially fighting a losing battle against nature.

Consistent exercise also makes the body intuitively crave the fuel foods of complex carbohydrates—potatoes, starches, and pasta, healthy things like that—instead of the sugars and fats found in donuts, ice cream, and potato chips. Exercise helps us to want to eat better.

As with exercise, good nutrition needs to be consistently practiced to do us much good. The keys to remember are these: high volume, low fat, and balance. Think about it. How many baked potatoes could you eat in one sitting before you're full? One or two, perhaps?

How many candy bars could you eat in one sitting before you're full? As many as are in the package, right? If you eat baked potatoes until you're full you'll consume maybe one hundred calories, tops. In one candy bar you'll consume around two hundred and fifty calories, and you won't be full.

Go ahead and eat the candy bar. But eat it after you've eaten the potatoes.

I grew up in Texas, and they used to say, "Eat your steak but go easy on your potatoes." We used to associate bulk with fat. But we had it wrong. The belief was incorrect. Volume doesn't necessarily mean fat, and it doesn't mean calories. You can have a pound of chocolate cake, twenty-six pounds of cantaloupe, or sixteen pounds of peaches. It's your choice. The calories are the same.

Now that we've talked about preparing ourselves physically through exercise and nutrition, let's move to another response area that's more emotionally oriented.

FINANCES

You might wonder what finance has to do with emotion, but isn't it chiefly our emotions that come into play when we're dealing with finances? If we have our finances under control, then our emotions will be in better control as well, and vice versa. The world doesn't seem like such a threatening place when we're fiscally fit.

In a book called *Uncommon Cents,* author Lynn Robbins offers some interesting perspectives on how we often look at finances and how we *ought* to look at finances. He makes a list of "The Seven Deadly Myths About Money," and I think they make a lot of sense and should be included here.

Consider the seven myths and their corresponding principles:

Myth 1: More money will solve my money problems.
  Principle: Greater income than outgo will solve my money problems.

Myth 2: Following a budget inhibits my freedom of choice.

Principle: Following a budget brings greater control over important choices.

Myth 3: The checkbook balance is my best spending barometer.

Principle: The checkbook balance cannot forecast the unexpected.

Myth 4: I spend according to my needs.

Principle: Most people spend according to emotion.

Myth 5: Going into debt gives me choices now instead of having to wait.

Principle: Going into debt decreases my future options.

Myth 6: Money is intrinsically valuable.

Principle: Money can only be exchanged for things of value.

Myth 7: My present financial situation is a result of circumstances and events out of my control.

Principle: My present financial situation is a result of decisions I made based on the money principles I believe in.

Robbins notes that this list isn't all-inclusive when it comes to money myths, but he gets his point across. Financial control is all about fitting principles onto our belief windows and then acting accordingly. It's when we fail to recognize our financial principles, or even know what they are, that we can get into financial difficulties. Applying time-proven principles ahead of time is preventive medicine that will eliminate the unnecessary stressors of financial concerns.

More Money Tips

One of my closest friends and a great mentor to me in life is Steven K. Scott, author of the book *A Millionaire's Notebook*. In his book,

Steve identifies additional correct principles regarding how to gain financial control of our lives. Consider a few of his principles:

1. Commitment and motivation are more important than credentials or resumes.
2. Do everything you can to make those you work with successful.
3. Make those under your authority successful, and you'll get an incredible ride on top of their rocket.
4. If it's not fun, you probably won't succeed, and any other way of getting rich is a waste of life.

When we're free of financial constraints, and we're exercising properly and regularly, we're in better shape to turn our attention to those significant people around us with whom we seek to have enduring, satisfying and, in some cases, lasting relationships.

RELATIONSHIPS

This is another area that has a tremendous impact on us emotionally. In understanding relationships, it's helpful to understand the concept of value. Most of us have a misconception about value. We've bought into the idea that value is intrinsic, that worth is innate; it will always be there. In the common view, value is seen as some kind of inherent quality that exists in a person, item, process, or service. After all, isn't gold intrinsically valuable? But in reality, value is not something intrinsic or innate at all. Value is achieved only through a complementary exchange of satisfaction of needs.

In applying this understanding to relationships, we can realize the importance of a *value exchange*. Only when there is a healthy exchange of values in both directions can there be a healthy relationship.

We cannot underestimate the need for relationships. Think about it. All of our needs are primarily met through relationships. Whether the need is for food, love, or to feel important, other people are most often relied upon to help us meet these needs. It's when these needs are met that relationships have value.

You establish a marriage relationship because you receive more value by being married than by being single. It enhances your life. It makes it better. There's real value there. Likewise, you have the same garage service your car every time because you value that the repairs are done right at a fair cost, or even because you value the convenience of the garage's location. Whatever, you have a *relationship* with the people who operate that garage, and it will be a relationship you'll only want to continue when it is of value to you.

It's when we fail to receive enough value that we question the need for relationships. Marriages end in divorce when there is no longer enough value being received, by one party or the other, or both. If you change garages it's because the quality declines or the prices become too high, or some other negative arises that decreases the value of that relationship.

By being aware of value, we can service our relationships better and be more conscious of the values we ourselves contribute. We will be motivated to work on skills of communication, intimacy, and selflessness. We will strive always to increase, not decrease, our value in our "valued" relationships, which will improve our mental and emotional stability.

MENTAL AND EMOTIONAL STABILITY

Being generally mentally and emotionally stable gives us the basis for a solid life that isn't at the whim of outside forces we would otherwise have no control over. Only with a solid mental and emotional foundation can we deal with the obstacles of modern life and actually find the time to thrive.

Mental and emotional stability gives us something I view as very important—the time for valuable self-talks that we can use to enhance our self-worth. Refer to this list of "A Dozen Affirmations" to keep you on the right track in regard to positive self-talking:

1. I am a valuable, kind person; I am worthy of the respect of others.
2. I am my own best friend; I nurture myself with exercise, healthful nutrition, and effective time management.
3. I enjoy my own company; I have a good sense of humor and can forgive myself when I make errors.
4. I love myself unconditionally; by loving myself I will have love to give to others.
5. I accept compliments easily and give them to others with ease.
6. I allow myself to feel my feelings and express them in healthy ways.
7. I set my goals clearly. I accept any setbacks as opportunities to learn as part of the process of my growth.
8. I hear, see, and believe in all that is positive, healthy, and helpful to myself and others.
9. I know negative thoughts and feelings deprive me of productive energy; I choose to be positive and productive.
10. I am compassionate, kind, truthful, and patient with myself and others.
11. I focus on that which I can directly control; I let go of worry and the things I cannot control or change.
12. I have plenty of time; I am organized, productive, and aware of my priorities.

Life Is Full of Negatives

If we subscribe to this list on a daily basis, the goal of mental and emotional stability can't help but be squarely in our sights. We can counteract the bombardment of negatives thrown at us daily. The *Wall Street Journal* recently published a report that said that every day by two in the afternoon school-aged kids had already received an average of 118 negative impressions about themselves. Like it or not, that's the kind of society in which we live. It's full of negatives. We hear them all the time, about ourselves, about others. Where are we if we don't have a personal course of preventive medicine that counters with at least an equal number of positive impressions?

I would like to add a personal endorsement to number three on the list above, specifically the part about humor. I believe a healthy sense of humor can be one of the best preventive medicines we can prescribe for ourselves. It's instructive that doctors have discovered a direct correlation between the immune system and a sense of humor. Norman Cousins is famous for his book *Anatomy of an Illness,* in which he describes having a degenerative disease and getting healthy again by taking vitamin C and watching funny videos.

We need to pay close attention to how much and how often we laugh. Studies show that the average child laughs four hundred times a day. The average adult laughs sixteen times a day. That's a serious decline, and for our own good it ought to be reversed. Laughter enhances our self-esteem; it boosts our sense of well-being. We should look for opportunities genuinely to laugh. We should make that a priority. We should associate with people who laugh and who help us see the humorous side of life. We should study children more and see what it is they have that we might have lost along the way.

The more pleasantly we view life, the more we'll have a yearning for creativity and expression.

CREATIVITY AND EXPRESSION

This is the last of the areas we want to cover in our look at preventive behaviors. It's the area that prompts us to focus inward and ask the following questions of ourselves:

- What do I really want?

- What activities have value for me?

- What do I really enjoy doing and sharing?

- What was I doing and how was I acting the last time I felt a complete sense of harmony and inner peace?

These questions are neither quickly nor easily answered. But pondered objectively they can help us understand what we want out of life and what excites us. As a result, we'll have a desire to become ourselves, rather than what others, or our environment, want us to be.

This "conformity to self" can be a real prison break. We'll stop conforming to other people's values and conform to our own values. We'll satisfy ourselves and not spend all our time trying to satisfy expectations that others may have for us.

We've all noticed that some people seem to have a certain magic in their approach to life. They have the uncanny ability to be at the right place at the right time and are always falling into opportunities and successes seemingly by accident while the rest of us watch in disbelief and frustration. That frustration is only heightened when these people don't seem to be at all aware of what they're doing. They casually stroll up and grab the brass ring we've been knocking ourselves out trying to get.

CONFORM TO YOURSELF

The secret to understanding those who seem to have the magic lies in applying the principles of conformity. Very likely they have bought into their own beliefs, their own values, and not someone else's. They realize they are unique. Not feeling a need to conform to anyone other than ourselves—within reason of course—can open up doors of creativity and expressiveness previously locked. We're at our best when we're ourselves, when we're aware of our own uniqueness.

Once we're aware of our own uniqueness we're in a much better position to balance all of the conflicting goals, needs, desires, and duties inherent in our lives. Balance is a key preventive behavior. With true balance in our lives we feel even further in control, and we're able to fill our many roles with a higher level of personal satisfaction. It is possible to be good spouses, good parents, good sons and daughters, good employees, good supervisors, good club members, good church members, and good taxpayers all at the same time. But only if we understand the need to balance. An overemphasis on any of the priorities in our lives can lead to an "out-of-round" life that satisfies some needs at the expense of others. We can't be two places at once. We can't invent more time. We can't be all things to all people.

Knowing what our human capabilities are and attending to them accordingly makes us masters and not slaves. Behavior can either lead, or it can follow. In the case of the addictions we talked about previously, it's a matter of behavior following the addictions. In the case of the measures of preparation talked about in this chapter, it's a matter of behavior leading the way to satisfactory results.

Instant Replay

Key Points

- A healthy lifestyle is preventive medicine.

- Preventive measures fit into these five categories: fitness and nutrition, finances, relationships, mental and emotional stability, and creativity and expression.

- Only exercise on days that you eat.

- Believe it or not, we *can* control money.

- Relationships work when there is an exchange of values.

- Positive self-talks can do wonders to drown out the negativity of the world.

- Don't conform to others, conform to yourself!

Personal Exercise

- Identify a financial myth currently operating in your life. Make a list of specific behaviors you can do to live by a time-proven principle.

- Check your Humor Quotient (see appendix).

- Keep an Exercise Log (see appendix).

- Keep a Personal Food Record (see appendix).

Where Do We Go from Here?

In chapter eight, we'll look at choices in a new light—not as something we have to do, but as something we *get* to do.

The Choices Are All Ours

If you can find a better path, take it! Each of us makes the decisions about where we want to go and how we want to get there. It's up to us and no one else.

By implementing preventive behaviors as outlined in the previous chapter, there's a marvelous side benefit that comes as a result of our resultant new control: We are able to really get in touch with what we want most.

It's a process of self-awareness, and it goes in orderly steps. Recognizing warning lights is the first step. By getting in touch with the appropriate signals we're moving in the right direction. Then comes preventive behavior. That's followed by a keener awareness of who we are, where we are, and, most important, where we want to go.

Once we know where it is we want to go, we put ourselves in a position to choose the right paths. When there is no destination, or when the destination is hazy at best, our choices of pathways don't amount to much more than the flip of a coin. As the saying goes, "No wind favors he who has no destined port." How many people spend their days walking around in circles, winding up at the end of the day at the exact same spot they found themselves the day before? Or even in a worse spot? How many addictions keep us from going anywhere except where we've already been?

LINDBERGH'S LANDING

The solo trans-Atlantic airplane flight of Charles Lindbergh stands as one of the most famous events in aviation history, and not because of Lindbergh's takeoff on May 20, 1927, at 7:52 A.M., from an airplane hangar at Roosevelt Field in New York. The reason Lindbergh and his plane, the *Spirit of St. Louis,* are legendary is because of the *landing* he made at Paris's Le Bourget airport thirty-three hours and thirty-two minutes later. It's the destination that put everything in focus. Lindbergh knew that just taking off wasn't good enough, and, in fact, without meticulous planning, it could have been disastrous. He knew he had just enough fuel, and he hoped enough endurance, to make it to that exact touchdown spot in France. His flight plan was direct and to the point. No detours. No side trips. From the moment he left New York he knew where he was going, and everything he did along the way was designed to keep the journey going in a straight line. He became famous because he knew where he was going. And that's precisely where he wound up.

Of course that's an easy example with both a tangible start and a tangible finish. Most of the destinations in our own lives—the things we want most—aren't tangible like that. Rather, they are ideals and goals that guide and shape our lives. They are those motivators that keep us excited and enthused about living. Intangible as they might be, we can nonetheless fix on our goals as tightly as Lindbergh fixed on Paris.

To me, the great golfer Jack Nicklaus serves as an excellent example of goal-focusing in the sports-minded twentieth century. I was watching an interview once when a reporter asked Nicklaus, who at that point had won nineteen major golf championships in his career, if he knew where he stood in relationship to the all-time greats of golf. Nicklaus had just finished his round that day and was, I presumed, off to dinner or to relax, and perhaps that's why I remember his answer so well. He didn't just give a short reply and hurry on as is usually the case in such situations. He pondered the question and then affirmed that, yes, as a matter of fact he knew *exactly* where he stood in relationship to the all-time greats of golf. He knew that Bobby Jones had won thirteen major championships, Ben Hogan had won eleven, Byron Nelson had won ten, and Arnold Palmer had won eight. He knew that his nineteen amounted to more than anyone in history, but he also knew that didn't mean somebody wouldn't come along some day and surpass what he had done. In fact, he said he fully expected that would happen, and he wouldn't be surprised if it happened in his lifetime. It was his belief that now that he had come along and taken Bobby Jones's mark and extended it into a further orbit, it would give the next generation a higher target to shoot at.

I thought Jack Nicklaus revealed two significant things that day about himself and about goal-setting:

One, his career had not been built on chance and happenstance. From the day he won his first major championship, at the age of twenty-two, up to that very moment, he knew what he wanted most. And he'd devoted all the energy he could to getting it.

Two, he knew the value of having a target in sight. He knew the importance of having something to shoot at, a verification that what you're aiming at is indeed reachable.

This interview was when Nicklaus was in his mid-forties, his prime playing days supposedly well behind him. I remember thinking as he concluded that interview that he just might win another major championship if he could, just to push that orbit out a little further and make it more of a challenge for those following in his wake. It was obvious that winning majors was his passion. That goal was still in front of him. That's what drove him. That's what kept him energized. A year later, when at the age of forty-six Jack Nicklaus became the oldest man to ever win the Masters and, in the process, run his list of major championship wins to twenty, I was not surprised. This was a man who knew where he was going and what he wanted most, and as a consequence got it.

As a postscript, I might add that I was also not surprised when Jack Nicklaus turned fifty not long after winning that Masters and showed little enthusiasm for the Senior Golf Tour. He really had no incentive for the senior tour because it offered him no path to the goals he had so firmly entrenched in his mind. They don't play major championships on the senior tour.

DIRECTION FROM WITHIN

Our pursuits may not be so famous or public as Charles Lindbergh's or Jack Nicklaus's, and certainly not as one-dimensional, but that doesn't mean they aren't as meaningful and as lofty. The idea behind destinations and goal-setting is they give our lives direction from within. They're meaningful and lofty because of their importance to us. If we view them as important, then they are important. It's as simple as that.

Diana Thornton is a management and professional development trainer with MCI, the telecommunications company headquartered in Atlanta. In talking about individual goal-setting, she likes to tell about her own experience at making choices and balancing her life's goals. When Diana first began working at MCI she immediately noticed a particularly strong work ethic that was an integral part of the company fabric. People came early and stayed late, and they worked hard. There was an unspoken company belief that said your face should be the first one the boss saw in the morning and the last one your boss saw at night; that you didn't go home until your "in" box was empty. Dutiful employees naturally adopted that company belief as their own.

Now this was fine for company productivity and on-the-job enthusiasm, and MCI thrived as a result. But Diana did not. She'd come to MCI from a nine to five job that had given her plenty of time to do the daily exercises that had become an important part of her life. Running and working out were very meaningful to her—as meaningful as her career. So she had a conflict on her hands. She had a strong professional work ethic of her own and wanted to be as successful as the company she had joined. She also didn't want to give up her physical exercise.

Such a time conflict might have frustrated her for years and made it difficult for her to enjoy either her new job or her exercising. But because Diana was trained in this material and hence tuned in to principle-driven behavior, she was able to work out a schedule that satisfied both her strong work ethic and her strong desire to work out. She knew she wouldn't be happy unless she was true to her beliefs and felt like she was working toward satisfying all of her goals. She decided that she would allow enough time for her daily workouts and not feel guilty if that meant the boss was still in his office when she left at night, or if her "in" basket wasn't entirely cleaned out. To compensate, she would come in earlier in the morning when she had to, and she would concentrate on being especially time-effective during her work day. She wouldn't be so inflexible that if a work conflict came up she wouldn't shift her workout schedule or cancel it altogether.

She Charted Her Own Path

Most important, she determined she would not feel guilty when she left work earlier in the day than others. She knew that her daily exercise was valuable to her in a lot of ways and that included giving her the energy she needed to be a more effective trainer. She wouldn't worry about what others were thinking because she was driven by beliefs that were correct for her, beliefs that she knew gave her feelings of self-worth and inner peace and would make her a better employee. Diana made her choices from within, not from without—and they worked, for her. She decided what direction she would go in based on her own values, not the values of others. The distinction is significant.

Direction should not be confused with rigidity. Our lives needn't be conservative straight lines, never deviating, always on a fixed course. In fact, well-roundedness demands exactly the opposite. Getting caught up in the "one goal" syndrome is a hazard we should be aware of and take great care to avoid. In truth, our lives are many-faceted, and as we seek to fill our basic needs, we are required to fill many roles. The important thing is to focus and concentrate on those facets and those roles that constitute for us a healthy, balanced life.

WHAT IS VALUABLE TO *YOU*?

Take a minute to jot down a list of those things that you personally believe are essential to a healthy and balanced life. In general terms, such lists typically include such things as meaningful relationships, professional satisfaction, an acceptable level of education, excellent health, things to look forward to (vacations, etc.), and quality time for favorite recreational pursuits and hobbies.

Now think of these items in Reality-Model terms. Are they needs, beliefs, rules, behaviors, or results?

When I ask this question at seminars, more often than not I'll get responses that these things are rules or results and sometimes even behaviors. I know this is something of a trick question, since any of these answers could be correct depending on your definition. The correct answer in this instance is that they are beliefs. How can I be so sure they're beliefs? Because that was what was asked for in the first place. Remember, I asked for a list of those things you personally *believe* are essential to a healthy and balanced life.

In other words, your list is what you *believe* you want most in your life. Using Franklin Covey time management terms, we would call these beliefs "values." Values are simply people's views about how they can best meet their needs *over time*. It's just a perception, but it's a powerful perception because it's based on your life's experiences.

Could you have incorrect values? Yes! Over time you may find that what you identified as a value today wound up driving behavior that didn't meet your needs over time.

When you build your personal "productivity pyramid" and identify your values, I believe it's important to make sure you have values that relate to and meet all four of your needs. If you do not have values established for one or more of your needs you will lead an unhealthy and unbalanced life. How many people do you know who are one dimensional and lament what's lacking in their lives? They may spend all their energy on a relationship, on their job, or on a hobby because they never focused and established a value in other areas of their lives. It's important that all our needs are addressed.

Remember, life's experiences are all we have to go by when establishing our values and beliefs. We get them from our parents, from the society we live in, from our surroundings, from our churches. In sum, we get our values and beliefs from whatever we're exposed to all of our lives.

OUR VALUES ARE OUR DESTINATIONS

It's these values and beliefs that become our destinations. They become what we want most. By being in touch with them (the closer the better) not only are we able to choose the right paths, but the obstacles in our lives, instead of being nothing but useless distractions, actually make a transformation and become what we view as *necessary* distractions.

If we're secure that the paths we're following fit into our beliefs, then following those paths will be valuable to us, threats, obstacles, and all. If the paths we're following don't fit into our beliefs, it only follows that we'd want to quit following them.

A good example is our jobs. We choose to work where we're working because we believe it will maximize our circumstances to achieve what we want most in life. That needs to be a given for us. It's our choice. If we don't believe where we're working is maximizing our potential, why work there? Lee Iacocca says if you can find a better car, buy it. I say if you can find a better path in your life, take it. Get off the path you're on now and get on a better one if you have a better one available to you. The point is it's our decision, and what we choose is because of a belief that that choice will maximize what we want most in life.

A Major Change

This point hit home very poignantly for one man who had spent his life developing a reputation as the hardest worker at his company. He was an ironworker, and he worked at two speeds: fast and faster. His job was his life. If there was a chance for overtime—and there usually was—he was the first to volunteer. He routinely worked Saturdays and Sundays. When he would finally go home, he would work on his house or his cars. He only stopped to eat and sleep and sometimes just barely. Every year his allotted vacation time went unused.

As you might assume, this devotion to work brought with it some casualties. His first marriage had dissolved, and his second marriage was on shaky ground. He'd developed very poor relationships with his children, and the same thing was happening all over with his grandchildren.

Then this hardworking ironworker was introduced to the Reality Model's concept of principle-driven behavior. For the first time in his life, after more than thirty-five years of hard work, he looked at the choices he was making and, more significant, at the beliefs driving those choices. During the course of his examination he came to the conclusion that he had a belief on his belief window that said you had to work constantly in order to provide for your family. Further examination revealed that this belief was a result of an upbringing during the Great Depression, when his father and mother worked almost around the clock to keep their family clothed and fed.

That hard-work belief had been strongly imprinted on this man's mind, and it drove his choices to work hard even if it meant sacrificing virtually every other area of his life. By being true to this belief, he'd succeeded in satisfying his need to live. No one could argue that. But it was at the exclusion of too many other needs.

He changed his belief to one that said hard work was important only to a point and that families needed to be provided for in more ways than financially. He cut back to forty hours a week. He turned down overtime. He took every minute of vacation time he had coming. He went places with his family and left work behind. Those were his new choices, and they were choices driven by his new belief. It wasn't easy at first. Hard work can be a very compelling habit. As he cut back he found that the results were as dramatic as they were positive. His marriage improved. He developed relationships with his grandchildren he had never enjoyed with his own children when they were young, and he mended fences with his children as well. All because he'd gone through the Reality Model and found his values and beliefs were out of whack. The plan he put together, based on his new beliefs, adjusted all that, and he found a peace and contentment he'd never known before.

We all have different circumstances. We need to look at them, whatever they might be, and take care to make sure our choices maximize what we want most in our lives. We should select our jobs based on that. We should select where we live, and how, based on what's best for our needs. Then we have ownership for where we're working and what we're doing. If you've got something better to do, do it. If you want to live off the land, then get out of the city; go do it. Don't complain about all the stuff you have to put up with every day as a result. It's your life, it's your choice. You chose it because it brings you certain benefits.

For example, I routinely ask people in my seminars who has the longest commute to work. After identifying the winner, I ask them, "Why do you commute so far?" The reasons are because they can live in a more desirable neighborhood, in a rural setting, or because it's closer to family. The point is, even though traffic is a stressor, it's OK with them because of the benefits that accompany it.

The key is to focus on the benefits and on making good choices, not on the obstacles.

I think it's important to note that ownership doesn't necessarily mean having some kind of physical title. It's a mental freeing up, a crystal clear perception that we're in charge of what we're doing.

EVERYONE FEELS LIKE AN OWNER

One of the biggest success stories in American business annals is the Marriott Corporation. What began as an A&W Root Beer stand in Washington, D.C., in 1927, has grown into one of the world's largest and most profitable food service and lodging corporations. Marriott hotels circle the globe, and the Marriott food services arm is ever-present, catering to airlines, businesses, and corporations.

A couple of years ago, after being named Chief Executive of the Year by a national magazine, the CEO of the Marriott Corp, J. Willard Marriott, Jr., son of the empire's founder, credited any success Marriott has had to a firmly held company principle that every employee would be treated as if he or she owned the company.

"My father started the tradition," said J. Willard Marriott, Jr., "by knowing the names and family histories of every employee." While the junior Marriott admitted that, with over 200,000 employees, that wasn't literally possible any more, the principle still held.

"We're still a family," he said. "Our mandate is the same now as it was in the beginning: Treat the employees in ways that cause them to create extra customer service. We want to take care of our employees so that they will want to take care of our customers."

The Marriott CEO shared a few of the principles his father handed down. They included:

- My greatest resource is my staff. If I stop listening, they stop talking, and then I lose their input.

- You can't manage a business by sitting in an office.

- Letting your employee know you care has to be part of your daily life, not just something you do once in a while.

- Don't forget the basics. Don't cook the pancakes in advance and put them on the steam table.

- The greatest reward you can give an employee is a pat on the back and telling them they're doing a good job.
  "We've found that money is well down the list of criteria for job satisfaction," said Marriott.

The above is no doubt why the Marriott Corporation, still a family-owned business, has done what most family businesses do not do—survived the second generation.

Marriott employees may be just that—employees—but they're treated as if they own the place.

OWNERSHIP HAS ITS PRIVILEGES

It's important to feel that sense of ownership. The beauty is, once we've established ownership, once we've put ourselves in charge, we can deal with what we have to deal with. If we don't assume that ownership we're doomed before we start. We're going to be constantly stressed out, frustrated, and disappointed. Struggles will be the norm. It will always be what everybody else is doing to us. Others will be to blame. We can't buy a break. Life won't be fair, and on and on.

When we assume ownership, then we look at the same things that might have stressed us out and frustrated and disappointed us in the past, and now we see them as part of the process to obtain what we want most in our lives. When that's the case, we can put up with the threats and the obstacles. We can work with them because we know they're along the path to our destination, and that's our choice. That's what we've decided to do.

Instant Replay

Key Points

- To choose the right path, we need to first know where it is we want to end up.

- All of our circumstances are different; choose paths that will maximize whatever your circumstances happen to be.

- When we're in touch with our needs, our choices will always be directed toward satisfying those needs.

- If you can find a better path, take it!

Personal Exercise

Make a list of the elements of a healthy balanced life (what you want most in life). Are you on a path (personally and professionally) to achieve what you want?

Where Do We Go from Here?

In chapter nine, we'll unveil the control continuum—a graphic device designed to help us consider what we can control and, just as important, what we can't.

Control What You Can and What You Can't

Once we have chosen our lives' paths, we are then in a better position to control our *responses* to obstacles we find on those paths by implementing correct beliefs.

How we handle the necessary obstacles and threats in our lives—the ones we've decided we'll accept and deal with as part of the process to meet our needs—is determined by the degree of control we have over those events. We need to always keep in mind that if any given event or obstacle is not part of the path that maximizes our circumstances, we need to eliminate it from our lives. It's the remaining events we need to learn to deal with.

Again, understanding is the key. In this case, understanding where the events in our lives fit into what we'll call the control continuum. The control continuum (please see accompanying illustration) helps us divide our lives' events into three categories: The first category is for those events that we have little or no control over, the second category is for those obstacles we have partial control over, and the third category is for those obstacles we have total or almost total control over. Obviously, the borders that separate these three categories are soft ones. With some obstacles it's hard to decide exactly where they belong while with others we find they're about halfway between categories, and we could accurately say that they belong to both.

The Control Continuum

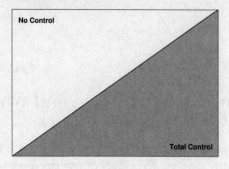

No Control

Total Control

THE CONTROL CONTINUUM

The control continuum allows us to see graphically just where the obstacles in our lives lie in terms of our control over them. If we'll each take our master list of events or obstacles and place them individually where we think they belong on the continuum, we can get a grasp on which ones should be getting our attention when it comes to control and which ones shouldn't.

It sounds elementary, and it is, but it's imperative that we know how much control we have over a given obstacle before we try to control that obstacle. If we have absolutely no control, then it follows that it's fruitless, not to mention depressing and a waste of time, to try to exercise any control. Conversely, if we have total control, then it's expedient that we exercise that control. To not do so wouldn't be in our best interest.

Let's take an example, using, once again, "the boss." Where on the control continuum do we put the boss? Well, it depends on the boss, of course. Very rigid, authoritative bosses would fit very close to the edge of the "no control" side of the continuum while bosses who delegate a lot of authority might fit squarely in the "partial control" section. Some bosses might even fit into the "total control" category, but probably only if you're somehow related to them.

For the sake of this example, let's say that we have a boss who is very rigid and demanding and one we don't think respects our opinions very much. So we've decided to put him or her in the "no control" category of the control continuum. That done, we might say, "so what?" If the boss isn't controllable by us, then what does it matter where we put him or her?

It matters because when we know how much control we have, we can then act—or not act—accordingly.

If we have absolutely no control over the boss, why would we ever want to beat our heads against the wall *trying* to have some control over him or her? It's good that we realize we have no control. We need to know that so we won't try to exert any.

Keep in mind that our job is a given. We've chosen to do what we do because we have decided it is the best path available to us to maximize what we want most in our life. We believe that. That's our decision. We're willing to deal with any *necessary* obstacles that might be associated with our job. Since we've decided that the boss is one of those necessary obstacles, and we've further decided that the boss is totally out of our control, the only way we can coexist peacefully with the boss is to accept our limitations. We can't control the boss so let's not try. Let's not waste our time and make our lives anxious and frustrated as a result.

PARTIAL CONTROL

Let's take another example. This time we'll use our old friend, "traffic." Let's say we decide that traffic, whether we like it or not, is an obstacle we can only partially control. So we'll put it in the middle of the control continuum. We've decided there are some things we can do about traffic, at least to a point. For starters, we could commute to work before or after rush hour. We could find another route home that's less crowded. We could buy foreign language tapes and listen to them while stuck in traffic, thereby turning a negative into a positive.

We could buy a car phone so traffic tie-ups wouldn't cut into our productivity as much. Those are all things we could decide to do that are under our control.

But we can't drive other people's cars, and we can't make other people carpool and leave their cars home. We don't have control over somebody cutting in front of us on the freeway, not using their turn signals, or driving slow in the fast lane. We can drive ourselves crazy (no pun intended) *thinking* we can make decisions for other people about their driving habits, but in reality that's their control, not ours.

So we've thought about it, and we've got a pretty good idea where our control starts and where it stops in regard to traffic. Now what? We accept both sides, that's what. We control what we can control, and we leave alone what we can't. The obstacle is identified, quantified, and actualized. That done, now the threat of traffic won't surprise us every day; it won't set our teeth on edge, and it won't ruin our day, because we know what to expect. We're prepared to control what we can and not worry about what we can't.

Ramifications Everywhere

Determining our degree of control and living with it has ramifications in all areas of our lives. Let's take "housecleaning" as another example. Many women who work outside the home can relate to the challenge of housecleaning when it comes to the area of partial control. I know one very successful career woman who for years found herself continually frustrated about her house not being as clean as the one she grew up in. Her mother, who did not work outside of the home, had been a very immaculate housekeeper. Her house was spotless. You could eat off the floors in her house. You couldn't find dust with a microscope in her house.

To compound the situation, this career woman married a man whose mother's house had been, if anything, even cleaner than her own mother's house had been. As a result, this woman felt a constant pressure to keep a clean house even though her career required that she spend her days away from home. She was frustrated, often angry, and was constantly nagging her husband and children to help her keep the house clean. She would come home from work and become a cleaning machine. She would ask the kids to pick up their things, and then she'd follow behind them picking up what they'd overlooked. In her own words she was not "a happy camper," and everyone around her knew it.

Only when she took another look at what she was doing and the degree of control she had over the situation was she able to relieve her frustration. First she reviewed the belief that was driving her behavior. She had a belief, she realized, on her belief window that said a disorderly house meant a bad wife and mother. It was a reflection on *her*. So every time she saw a messy house she transferred that to her self-worth.

But if she *changed* that belief to fit her lifestyle, and not her mother's or her mother-in-law's, it could meet her needs. She did just that. Her new belief became "A disorderly house means a busy family with more important things to do."

That done, her next step was accepting the fact that she only had partial control over how much picking up others would do (and less than partial control if the others happened to be teenagers). She could control her own housecleaning, of course, and her new belief actually gave her more control over herself—now that her new belief gave her new standards that didn't call for a floor clean enough to eat off of.

This woman went so far as to line up her family in the living room one night to *announce* that there was going to be a behavior change. The family members, as we'd all guess, were happy about the behavior change, and so was the mom. The house actually became tidier as a result, and frustration and anger went out the window. Understanding that you can't have total control over the cleanliness of your house if you're not there all the time turned out to be a very valuable realization.

TOTAL CONTROL

How about those things over which we have total control—such as where we're going to eat, how we want to balance our work time with our family time, or any of a hundred other things we could list? The answer is simple. If we have total control, then exercise total control. If we don't, we'll have no one to blame but ourselves. What does Nike say? Just Do It!

Let me share with you a study by Dr. Raymond Flannery of the Harvard Medical School. In his research on human behavior, Dr. Flannery found four characteristics common to what he called "stress-resistant" people. The first characteristic of these enviable people was that they took charge. If something came up they would find a way to control it if they could. If they needed something to be fixed, they'd fix it. If they needed some information on some topic, they'd go to the library and get that information. These people were in charge—in sharp contrast, Dr. Flannery found, to less stress-resistant people who would typically control almost nothing, most of the time choosing to look to others for help. Their first reaction when given an assignment was to ask as many people as possible to assist them.

The second characteristic of stress-resistant people that Dr. Flannery found was that these individuals knew what they wanted most. They had meaning and direction and purpose in their lives. Their goals were well defined, their courses well charted. These were people who were fixed on specific points and followed the paths that would get them there.

The third characteristic was a healthy lifestyle. Eighty percent of these stress-resistant people engaged in regular aerobic exercise as compared to only 20 percent of those more susceptible to stress. A healthy lifestyle also included taking time for active relaxation, on an average of ten to fifteen minutes a day. These people watched what they ate. They knew what was good for them and what wasn't.

The fourth characteristic was they had a friend, a buddy, someone they could trust and talk to: somebody they could release with; someone to share the lows with and the highs.

Incidentally, a "friend" doesn't have to necessarily be human. Having "someone to talk to" doesn't absolutely require that they talk back. Pets can be valuable tools in resisting stress. A recent study done by the University of Buffalo Medical School revealed that pets were more effective than spouses when it came to helping keep blood pressure and heart rate down during stressful testing.

In the study, 240 married couples were asked to perform three stressful tests, first with a spouse present, then with a dog present. Overall, physical signs of stress were highest with the spouse there. In one task that involved math problems, the study showed heartbeats rising an average seven beats a minute higher with the dog present and thirty-seven beats a minute higher with the spouse present. Diastolic blood pressure rose eight milligrams with the dog and twenty-six milligrams with the spouse!

The study concluded that we perform better when we don't feel the pressure of evaluation—a pressure we don't get from man's (and woman's) best friend.

Being in Charge

Using the Harvard study as evidence, it seems safe to conclude that stress resistance is best realized when we make our own (calculated) choices, employ the wonders of preventive medicine, socialize effectively, and, finally, take control of our lives; and that includes control—in an interesting kind of a twist—of those things we have no control over.

Modern stress maintenance, in essence, is a process of either controlling or flowing.

Flowing is what it sounds like it is. When the current is too strong to do anything about it, then flow with it.

In Ugh's stone-age times, flowing wasn't really an option. The saber-toothed tiger was Ugh's obstacle, and he couldn't really go up to the tiger and say, "Hey, chill out." Ugh had two choices: fight or flight. That's the way it is with physical threats. They require a physical response. But mental threats are different. They can be dealt with through a mental response. To mental threats we can fight, flee, or flow, and flowing (some people call it "rolling with the punches") is by far the most preferable. Flowing fights fire with fire, so to speak, or mental with mental. Flowing is a response driven by a principle on a belief window.

To be effective at flowing requires that we modify our beliefs, and the best way to modify our beliefs, as we've already discussed, is with self-talks. Let me suggest one self-talk—remember, self-talks are the triggers for our behavior—that I would highly encourage using in no-control situations. Simply ask yourself, "Is it worth it?" Is it worth all the negative mental, emotional, and physical effects it's capable of causing?

He Saved Lives by Flowing

One of the great examples of "flowing" in history is Oskar Schindler. The story of this real-life Robin Hood—first told in the book and then in the Academy Award–winning movie of the same name, *Schindler's List*—is a virtual clinic in flowing.

Oskar Schindler, a Catholic-born Czechoslovakian with a penchant for business, found himself in Krakow, Poland, when Nazi Germany occupied the country and took over its affairs. Instead of fighting against these invading dictators Schindler modified his business style so he could not only survive, but still turn a profit. Through bribes and diplomacy, he was able to get the Nazis to allow him to employ Jewish workers in his enamelware factory. This gave Schindler the manpower he needed for his factory, and it gave the Jews he employed, despite the fact that they lived in the very shadow of the Holocaust, a safe refuge.

By the time the war was over, Schindler was credited with saving the lives of 1,100 Jews, and he had maintained a successful business at the same time. At his death, he was given the "Righteous Gentile" award by the State of Israel and buried with honors in a Jerusalem cemetery.

As Oskar Schindler demonstrated, partial control over a situation can definitely be used to one's advantage as long as the boundaries are well known and well observed. Only control what you can.

RESPECT "NO CONTROL"

If we have absolutely no control over something, we need to respect that, too. If we get into a stress response over that something, in essence we're saying: "This is worth dying for," or at the least, "This is worth going through misery for." There are some things worth dying for, and I'm not saying there aren't. And there are some things worth getting upset or uptight or downright miserable over. But the vast majority aren't worth it. As the saying goes, "Don't sweat the small stuff—and it's all small stuff."

Often the problem is that our perception is worse than reality. We need to make sure our perceptions don't run so far away from reality that the two are on different planets, figuratively speaking, that we don't think something is worth dying for when it isn't. We can think a situation is catastrophic when in fact it is far from that. We can constantly imagine gloom and doom and pay considerably more attention to our perceptions than our realities.

Life Isn't Always Fair

Worse yet, we can allow ourselves to fall into the familiar "Life is supposed to be fair" trap. Believing that life is fair is one of the most dangerous beliefs we could ever apply to our belief windows. Life is not fair. On a realistic level, we all know that. We're all aware of handicaps that range from emotional to physical to economic that hit some of us harder than they hit others. Yet, if we're not careful, we can be lulled into thinking that somehow things are going to always be fair, and they won't be.

The biggest danger with a "Life is fair" belief is that the moment something unfair happens to us we are then susceptible to all the unhealthy responses. We'll be frustrated, anxious, angry, and irritable. We'll buy into all those reactions that take away our inner peace and eat away at us.

But if we develop a belief on our belief window that says there are unfair things that happen in life that are an integral part of existence and when they happen we'll deal with them the best we can, then we are in a position to maintain our balance and our physical, emotional, and mental health. This point was brought home to me when I was teenager and had just started to drive. I got in a minor fender bender as new drivers are wont to do, and I'll never forget coming home and having to face my dad to tell him I'd just wrecked the family car. I felt a lot of fear and trepidation as I approached my dad, anxious about what his response would be.

All my dad said was, "If you're not hurt, that's OK." He said we had insurance and not to worry about the accident, that those things happen. He taught me such a valuable lesson that day on how to respect that unfair things happen as a part of life. Sure, you want to do all you can, but sometimes even when it's not your fault you'll get in an accident. Those things happen.

I recently had a friend who got in a traffic accident and suffered a whiplash. Was it fair that some young teenage driver's reckless behavior unfairly caused a lot of pain and aggravation to an innocent person? Of course it wasn't fair. But those things happen. We can either let them destroy us, or we can take them in stride as part of the process of our life and as part of the path to maximize our circumstance. Remember, as unfair things happen to you they become part of your "new" circumstances. Rather than get upset at my new circumstance, the productive response becomes, "What can I do to max-imize my new circumstance."

LOOKING AT ASSETS

One of the best ways to keep perception and reality in close proxim-ity is to keep a firm grip on our individual assets. If we take a regular inventory of the positive things in our lives, that can be one of the best hedges against runaway fears and worries. A good way to take men-tal inventory is to create safety deposit boxes in our minds—to dwell on the things that *are* fair. At least for us.

I knew of a man who was very wealthy and very successful, but who was nonetheless constantly worried about how well the current project he was working on would turn out and, after that project was concluded, about what he would work on next. What if another proj-ect didn't come along? What if this current project was a bust? What if and what if and what if? He was a walking, talking, negative time bomb. Anxiety was a constant companion. They went everywhere to-gether. He fretted and worried all the time. He paid virtually no at-tention to the fact that during an already lengthy career he had piled up one success after another and was the envy of those around him. He was very talented and accomplished.

This man had access to a very positive resource that for much of his life he chose to ignore. That positive resource was his mental safety deposit box. Once he realized it was there and started paying regular visits, through self-talks, it produced exceptional dividends. Those visits revealed treasures he had kept well hidden from himself, trea-sures of great worth.

In his safety deposit box, he discovered he had more than enough money to take care of himself and his loved ones the rest of their lives, whether any additional money came in or not. He discovered he'd al-ready been successful at any number of projects, and those could never be taken away. What's more, he realized he'd always had enough projects to keep him as busy as he wanted to be, so why should that change now?

Once he became familiar with the whereabouts of his personal safety deposit box he got in the habit of visiting it often. Whenever those old negative thoughts of failure and insecurity arose, he would take a trip to visit his assets.

(See adjoining illustration for an example of a Safety Deposit Box filled in for the four needs areas.)

Your Safety Deposit Box

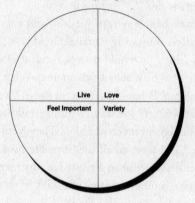

TAKE INVENTORY

You can likewise take your own inventory. See how many assets you can come up with. Remember that this is not just a financial safety deposit box. This is for all of the four needs: live, love, self-worth, and variety. Some questions that might help you identify your inventory include:

- What financial assets do I have should my current circumstances change?

- What skills do I have?

- What accomplishments am I particularly proud of?

- What personality traits really help me get through the bad times?

- What do I like about myself?

- What relationships make me feel good?

- Where are my safe places?

- What are my favorite things to do or share?

- Where would I like to be, with whom and doing what, on an ideal weekend?

- What kinds of risks do I most often take?

Put these answers in your safety deposit box and add anything else you can think of. How about pets? Your church? If you consider such things as assets in your life, put them in. If you have a close personal friend, a best buddy, that's a definite asset. Anything that makes you feel better about yourself or helps you in your life should be in your safety deposit box. A good sense of humor should definitely be listed as a valuable asset. What hobbies keep you interested in life? Find a spot for them in your box of assets.

Once you've taken your inventory, determine that you will go through this mental exercise on a regular basis. It's a most effective way for us to take positive stock of our lives. It's all based on reality. The more we put into our safety deposit boxes the less threatening those things we have little or no control over become. Imagining unfortunate events, such as being laid off from work or having to move, will become less threatening as we realize our stock of assets is sufficient to carry us through tough times.

The more we visit our mental safety deposit boxes, the better we'll think of ourselves and the more secure we'll feel. It can give us the kind of security that allows us to get outside of ourselves and help others who we might perceive as less fortunate. The average American has two clinically diagnosed episodes of depression between ages thirty-five and sixty-five. One of the best ways to treat depression is to help someone less fortunate than yourself. You can always find someone worse off. By helping them you feel better about yourself, you boost your self-esteem, and hence treat your own depression.

Taking a mental inventory can also help us identify those assets we don't have but would like to achieve. Once we feel comfortable that we are in control of a number of assets, adding to our "stash" will become easier and easier. We'll consider ourselves both wealthy and secure. We'll feel in control.

Instant Replay

Key Points

- It's as important to know what we can't control as what we can.

- Life is not fair. When unfair things happen to us they become part of our new circumstance.

- Events over which we have no control require us to flow.

- We flow by modifying beliefs on our belief window.

- We all have mental safety deposit boxes filled with our assets.

- Our assets in our mental safety deposit boxes determine if the threats in our lives are real or perceived.

Personal Exercise

- Fill in the control continuum to identify how much control you have over the obstacles in your life.

- Create a safety deposit box of your assets in your four need areas to identify if the threats in your life are real or perceived.

Where Do We Go from Here?

In chapter ten, we'll learn about a powerful tool we call the "Why Drill." Its purpose is to help us drill to the core of what's driving our behavior.

Why Ask Why?

When we were kids, we never stopped with the
questions; so why stop now? Asking why we behave
a certain way can help us identify the beliefs that
are driving us.

Children can be terrific role models in demonstrating how to deal
with life. One thing that children do particularly well is ask "why?"
Why does it rain? Why does the sun come up in the east and go down
in the west? Why do bees sting? Why do I have to go to bed?

We all used the "Why Drill" extensively as children. The reason
was simple: The "Why Drill" gave us answers. It was how we
learned. As we grow up we tend to put it on a shelf and not use it very
often, which is too bad. Effective use of the "Why Drill" allows us to
probe to the very core of what motivates and drives us. The "Why
Drill" is a most effective way to uncover our personal truths and beliefs and help us answer whether they are correct for us or not.

THE "WHY DRILL"

The need to use the "Why Drill" becomes quickly obvious once we
put it into practice. Too often the results of our behavior go
unchecked. We become creatures of habit. We do something today
because that's what we did yesterday. We don't ask for answers like
we did when we were children. Even when we're struggling, instead
of questioning, we tend to continue with the same repetitive behavior.

The "Why Drill" is valuable because it can help us identify why we're struggling. It does this by identifying incorrect beliefs. Remember, the definition of an incorrect belief is something that drives behavior that does not meet my needs over time. The first step to achieving our personal best is a clear identification of our incorrect beliefs—those beliefs on our belief windows that trigger behavior and results that don't meet our needs over time. Once we clearly identify incorrect beliefs, we're in a position to replace them with correct beliefs that do meet our needs over time.

The "Why Drill" is easy to use. There's no electricity necessary or any other power source beyond our own minds. If we simply start asking "why," we're instantly operational. We turn on the "Why Drill" simply by asking "why" questions about our behavior.

MY OWN EXPERIENCE

Let me use my own life's experience as an example. In earlier chapters I've already related my experiences as a lawyer and how I eventually left the practice of law because I determined it was not fulfilling my needs. It took a long time for me to make that change, and remember, that change didn't occur until the pain was great enough for me to do something about it. If I had known about the "Why Drill" and used it effectively, I could have saved myself a lot of that pain.

In seminars I'll ask the participants to go ahead and ask me any "why" questions they want about my behavior as a lawyer to identify the belief on my belief window and the need behind it that was driving my behavior.

Usually the first question asked me by the "Why Drill" is "Why did you choose law?"

"Well," I'll answer, "I chose law because I remember a distinct feeling from a very early age that if I was going to be looked up to when I got older, if I was going to be somebody important, I should be a doctor or a lawyer. Since there was a long tradition of law in my family, I chose lawyer over doctor."

The next "Why Drill" question will always be something like, "Why did you think being a lawyer or a doctor would make you important?"

My answer: "Because that's what people constantly told me. 'I hope you grow up to be a lawyer or doctor,' they'd say. Over and over again I heard about the esteemed status of lawyers. If I was a lawyer I would be respected, and people would think well of me." This was reinforced every time I observed someone meeting another person. They would introduce themselves, and then ask what they did for a living. As soon as they told them what they did they were immediately categorized. I could see this. I learned that people think more highly of you if you're in a "prestige" profession.

Often it will take more than two "why" questions to get to the belief on a belief window that drives behavior. But in this example, that's all it took. After hearing my response to just two questions it's safe to conclude the following:

1. I chose to practice law because the belief on my belief window is that others' perception of my job determines my self-worth.
2. The need threatened is my self-worth need.

The belief on my belief window goes way back to when I was a child—and an avid practitioner, I should add, of the "Why Drill."

It was the same with my early introduction to athletics. By employing the "Why Drill" it's not difficult to see why I shaped a belief on my belief window that beating other people was necessary for me to satisfy my self-worth need. Almost from the first time I participated in sports, that belief was reinforced. Every time I'd come back from a race what would people ask me? They'd ask me how I did. "Did I win?" If I said I did win they'd say, "Yeah, all right. Good job. Way to go. We're proud of you." On the other hand, if I said I lost they'd get a sympathetic look on their faces and say, "Oh, that's too bad! Better luck next time."

So winning is important, that's what I'd keep hearing. And what's winning? It's beating other people. You can't win and not beat other people. It's all relative. Success, praise, fame, and fortune are contingent upon finishing higher than other people. If that's what I believe, then that's what's on my belief window, and that's what will drive my behavior as I strive to satisfy my self-worth need.

When the "Why Drill" question is why do I feel winning is important, that's my answer. That's why.

APPLY THE NATURAL LAWS

The "Why Drill" wouldn't do us much good if we stopped here. Only when we apply important Natural Laws, or values, does it help us shape new beliefs to drive behavior that will result in change in our lives. In the case of the self-worth need—and that's the one that applies to my two personal examples I have given—I discovered the Natural Law to be this:

When my self-worth is dependent on something external, I will not meet my needs over time.

By "external" I mean, of course, anything outside my control. If I have a need dependent on something outside my control, that's going to leave me, sooner or later, *out of control*. And if I'm out of control, more often than not I'm going to be frustrated, anxious, incapable of making decisions, a reactor rather than a proactor.

If my self-worth is dependent on something internal then that changes everything, because now I'm *in control*. I'm in charge. If something's frustrating me or making me anxious it's within my power to change it. That makes all the difference in the world.

Again, using my personal examples with the law and athletics, my two original beliefs were based on things external. I believed I was only as important as how others perceived my profession. And I believed winning is beating other people. Both beliefs relied on other people's perceptions and behavior, not mine. Only when I changed to internal beliefs in both cases—that my profession was important if it was enjoyable and fulfilling to *me,* and that winning meant giving *my* best shot—was I able to have behavior driven by correct beliefs that met my self-worth need over time.

By using the "Why Drill," that becomes clear.

WORKPLACE EXAMPLE

Let's take an example from the workplace. Let's say you work for a company that makes a lot of management changes, and that disturbs you. Every time you get a new manager or boss you become insecure and confused because you're anxious about what this new person might expect and whether you'll meet their expectations. You don't like this. You don't want to be insecure and confused, of course; you want to be calm, confident, and at peace. But you don't have that.

So let's apply the "Why Drill" to the situation.

> FIRST QUESTION: "Why does it stress you out when the company changes your supervisors?"
>
> ANSWER: "Because supervisors are all different."
>
> SECOND QUESTION: "Why does it matter to you if supervisors are different?"
>
> ANSWER: "Because my new supervisor might want to make changes."
>
> THIRD QUESTION: "Why do you have anxiety about changes?"
>
> ANSWER: "Because *I* could be one of those changes."
>
> FOURTH QUESTION: "Why don't you want to be one of those changes?"

ANSWER: "Because I could be out of my job."

FIFTH QUESTION: "And why is it important to you that you keep your job?"

ANSWER: "Because it allows me to provide for myself and my family and because it contributes to my feelings of self-worth."

From these questions and answers, the "Why Drill" cuts to the heart of your belief that says "New supervisors do things differently, and I might not fit into their scheme of things." That being your belief, it's going to drive behavior that produces anxiety, insecurity, and confusion every time there is a management change. Since that kind of behavior produces results that do not meet your needs over time (your self-worth need will definitely be adversely affected and your insecure behavior could drive you right out of the job that's paramount in satisfying your need to live), you're now in position to look at the incorrect belief and change it to a correct belief. After you understand the "why," you can implement the change.

In our hypothetical case involving "management change," you'd want to change your belief from your initial external outlook (management means change, and I fear change) to an internal belief that would give you control.

You'd first want to assess what you don't have control over. In this case, you don't have control over the frequent management changes. If the company wants to make a lot of management changes it will make a lot of management changes. That being a given, you need to look at what beliefs will drive internal control. You need to come up with a new belief that, instead of generating an unhealthy response to something over which you have no control, will empower you to generate a healthy response to something you can control.

You need to realize that the situation, whatever it is, will happen again, and that when it does, it will be much more beneficial for you to be able to generate a different, healthy response.

THEORETICAL NEW BELIEF COMES FIRST

The first step is to come up with a *theoretical* new belief that when strongly imprinted will drive the behavior and responses that are really wanted and will meet your needs over time. You need to ask yourself, "What new theoretical belief can I live by that will drive new responses that will empower me to flow in a situation over which I have no control?" The reality of actually implementing this theoretical new belief will come later, and we'll discuss how to do that in detail in the next chapter. But first it's important to realize that the first step is to identify the theoretical new beliefs and firmly imprint them.

Continuing with our example dealing with a fear of "management change," how about a theoretical new belief that "My self-worth is based on how I deal with change to increase my skills and productivity"; and "New management creates new opportunities"? Both are internal. Both turn the frequent management changes into a positive instead of a negative. How about this new theoretical belief on your belief window: "If I do a quality job then that's all I can ask of myself, and I'll have peace and calm no matter what happens"?

Will that make management change less anxious and threatening? Of course it will. Even though nothing external will have changed, you will have—by modifying a belief on your belief window.

Along the way, of course, we'll also become a lot more tolerant of those around us. That's inherent with behavior that is inward looking and not outward looking. If we're not always telling people what they should be, narrow-mindedness will change to broad-mindedness. Expectations that we thrust onto others often set us up for disappointment. That doesn't mean we should approve or excuse rude behavior by other people. It means we should give other people enough space to allow them their own opinions and decisions. Appreciating the differences in others brings about workable, complementary solutions instead of adversarial relationships. All this is a byproduct of inward-oriented behavior driven by internal beliefs.

In other words, by looking *inside* we become our own best allies and not our own worst enemies.

THINK BEFORE YOU LEAP

There's a story I read in the newspaper a few years ago that I think illustrates this point very well, and very soberly. It involved a basketball player who was trying to make the roster of an NBA team. The player was a center, close to seven feet tall, and like all those invited to try out for the team he had been a star in college. He survived the early cuts and made it onto the team that would play in the exhibition season that preceded the regular season. He was very close to realizing his lifelong dream of playing professional basketball in the NBA.

When the team took its first road trip of the exhibition season, a problem arose. On the flight to the game, this player was assigned a seat in the coach cabin while the veteran players and several of the team's coaches and administrators sat in the first class cabin. As he sat in his coach seat, which had considerably less leg room than his seven-foot frame needed, the player got more and more frustrated. Adding to his frustration was the fact that the team's general manager was one of those he'd seen sitting in first class. He knew there was a rule in the standard NBA player's contract that said players were supposed to get airplane seat priority over noncoaches, and that included the general manager.

When the plane landed the player had had sufficient time to get incensed enough that he complained to the general manager over the inequity of the seating arrangements. He told him he wasn't happy about being treated unfairly and that on the return flight he expected that he and the general manager would switch seats. He'd be in first class and the general manager would be in coach.

You can probably guess what happened next.

The general manager told the player he could fly back in whatever seat he liked because as of right this moment he could consider himself no longer a member of the team!

There is no question that the aspiring NBA player was right in his interpretation of the rules. But he missed one key point. He wasn't on the team yet. He lost track of what he had control over and what he didn't have control over. This was a classic case of sacrificing what was wanted most (an NBA career) for what was wanted now (more leg room). If the college star had brought out the "Why Drill" as he sat in his coach seat instead of negative self-talks, he'd have played in that night's game and perhaps the next game and the one after that, until he was a full-fledged member of the team. Instead of brooding over what he *perceived* as mistreatment, he'd have first asked himself, "Why are you upset?" and before long he'd have concluded that the belief on his belief window was that he was a star, he'd always been a star (in junior high, high school, and college), and if he wasn't being treated like a star he wasn't respected. Armed with that knowledge, he'd have been able to reason that a better theoretical belief in his rather precarious situation would be something like, "I'm a rookie now, and all rookies, no matter who they are and how great they were in college, have to go through boot camp. Being treated like a rookie means I'm on the first step to a lengthy and satisfying career as an NBA basketball player."

He'd have gotten off the plane smiling as the circulation returned to his legs, and he'd have asked the general manager if he'd had a nice flight.

EXERCISE PRINCIPLES

For an outside-the-workplace example, let's use exercise. Let's say that you hate to exercise. Exercise for you is completely unpleasurable. You'd rather sit through the Ice Follies than exercise.

First, apply the "Why Drill."

FIRST QUESTION: "Why do you hate to exercise?"

ANSWER: "Because it's no fun."

SECOND QUESTION: "Why is it no fun?"

ANSWER: "Because it's boring, it takes too much time, and I don't get anything out of it."

THIRD QUESTION: "Why don't you feel like you get anything out of it?"

ANSWER: "Because it takes me away from the things I really enjoy doing."

Notice that in this "Why Drill" example the questions and answers are going in a circle. Before long, we'd be right back to the question "Why do you hate to exercise?" and the answer "Because it's no fun." That brings us, in a roundabout way, to the conclusion that you have a belief on your belief window that says either exercise should be enjoyable, or everything you do in your spare time should be fun and enjoyable. Somewhere in your life you've picked up that belief. Perhaps from the ads on TV for exercise equipment that feature smiling, fit models who act as if they're having the time of their lives (and never sweat). Or perhaps from friends who have talked glowingly of their "exercise highs." Or perhaps from a notion that you work hard when you're on the job, and everything else you do in your life is your reward for that hard work, and exercise is *not* a reward. You don't choose to use your free time in pain.

Whatever its origin, you have that belief—that exercise should be fun—and since every time you've tried to exercise you've found it no fun, you don't keep doing it, you have bad results, and the needs you're trying to meet aren't being met.

Once you understand "why," however, you're ready for a new theoretical belief, which might be along the lines of "The primary reason for exercise isn't to have fun, it's to take care of my body so I'll feel better, look better, and have more energy for the important things in my life." Or maybe "Exercise only becomes fun after I'm in sufficient shape to enjoy it."

To reinforce that new theoretical belief you might think about other examples of things you do, or have done, in your life that aren't necessarily "fun," but are still eminently worthwhile. Studying for a test in school, for example, or growing a garden. Those are things that take work before they yield results. As it is with them, so it is with exercise.

Armed with that new theoretical belief, you can imagine jumping on your stationary bike, your rowing machine, or your cross-country ski simulator and grinning and bearing the pain as you physically exert. Your new theoretical belief will trigger new visualized behavior, which in turn will generate results that will meet your needs. Again, in the following chapter we will discuss how to turn our theoretical beliefs into reality.

ALWAYS ADD THE WORDS "OVER TIME"

In any example we choose to use, remember that we have to add the words "over time" to our final analysis. Will the theoretical belief on my belief window drive behavior that will meet my needs *over time*? When the answer is in the affirmative, we know we have a theoretical belief that is correct for us.

The beauty of the "Why Drill" is that it can be used in all situations of our lives to help us focus on the beliefs that drive our behavior. Sometimes it can take a while to get to the belief, and sometimes the belief is quickly recognizable. Whatever the case, it's the accurate appraisal of that belief that frees us to change. We can't really find out anything until we start asking questions.

Besides working for us as individuals, the "Why Drill" can also be used effectively as we look at others we associate with—as was the case with the aspiring NBA basketball player—as well as situations in general in our lives.

For example, if we have a coworker who has a certain style of doing things, and that style doesn't exactly jibe with our style of doing things, exercising the "Why Drill" can help us understand the beliefs on our coworker's belief window that are driving his or her behavior. We can ask the "why" questions either silently to ourselves or directly to the other person, with sensitivity and diplomacy helping determine when to use either. There is great value that comes from understanding other people's beliefs. Once we understand what's driving others' behavior we're capable of either helping them with a change that might be helpful to them, or having much better empathy for the reasons they behave as they do. At the very least, we'll keep in touch with what we truly have control over, and we'll understand them and be able to predict their behavior.

LEARN FROM OTHERS

Sometimes we can learn valuable lessons from others who we realize are operating under correct beliefs.

I personally learned a very valuable lesson about management and coworkers from a close friend who introduced me to Franklin. His name is Kevin Hall. Kevin was the national sales and training director at Franklin, and he told me one of the reasons he wanted me to work for Franklin was because he liked to surround himself with "threatening" people. That sounded really strange to me, but when Kevin explained what he meant it really made sense. He said that if he hires only people who are accomplished and typically excel then not only will they make him a better person by helping him improve his personal talents, but think of what a quality organization he could build.

Kevin's belief worked! He surrounded himself with quality people who helped propel Franklin from a start-up company to a nationally known and highly regarded organization. Think how different the results would have been if Kevin's belief was "Hiring quality people threatens my job." Kevin would have kept himself in charge of a sales force that would never have amounted to much, just so he could ensure he'd never be threatened.

I see similar situations in the corporate world all the time where employees are afraid of losing their jobs to the extent that they'll undermine their own progress and the progress of their company, to maintain the status quo. Such a belief will not work "over time." Using the "Why Drill" in such situations would be of great value in helping to identify those incorrect beliefs that hold us back from where we want to be.

Instant Replay

Key Points

- We can identify incorrect beliefs by applying the "Why Drill."

- Once incorrect beliefs are identified, they should be substituted with theoretically correct beliefs.

- Our needs will not be met over time if they are based on external things.

Personal Exercise

- Look at different areas of your life (family, job, health) and identify your behavior patterns (habits) in each.

- Apply the "Why Drill" to identify what beliefs are driving those behavior patterns.

- Visualize new, better behavior patterns in those areas (how would you like your life to be?).

- Identify theoretical beliefs, which would drive those new behavior patterns.

Where Do We Go from Here?

In chapter eleven, we'll begin to look at specific ways we can implement new beliefs in our lives that will promote real growth.

Practice Makes Perception

Creating experiences—both actual and visualized—
is the secret behind imprinting new beliefs. You can't
believe what you haven't experienced.

Sam Snead, the legendary golfer, had a favorite expression he used whenever he played in Pro-Ams. "The trouble with most amateurs," he would observe, "is they never hit the ball with their practice swing."

His point was wry but apt. He'd watch a smooth, controlled practice swing as his amateur partner would warm up for the real thing. Then the real thing would come, and it would bear little or no resemblance to the practice swing. It would be at least twice as fast and twice as hard. And, unfortunately, it would yield roughly the same result as the thousands of too fast, too hard "real" swings that had preceded it.

In golf as well as most everything else, we are creatures of habit. We can *want* to do things differently. We can plot and plan and scheme to depart from the way we've performed in the past. Using golf as a case in point, we can pay for thousands of dollars of lessons, subscribe to all the top instructional magazines, spend hundreds of hours beating balls on the driving range, and buy all the latest clubs. We can learn what we're *supposed* to do, and we can really *want* to do it.

Then we come to the difficult part. We go to the first tee and play for real, and the hardest thing of all—a lot harder than paying for all those lessons—is to *really change our swing.*

HABITS AREN'T EASY TO CHANGE

Think about the way you live your life. Think about the habits you've reinforced over time, year in and year out. Those habits, good or bad, correct or incorrect, make up who you are and what you do. We *are* our habits, whatever they might be.

When I raced competitively I had my own way of running the steeplechase, my own game plan. It was unique to me. I would always start at the back of the pack, very often in last place. I did this for what I came to realize were two good reasons: One, by staying out of the pack I avoided all the early jostling and pushing that typically went on as the race proceeded past the various obstacles, hurdles, and water jumps. Two, over time I came to the realization that I had a decent kick that, if conserved properly, could carry me past the field on the final lap. If my pace was right, I knew I could count on enough sprint speed to make up the ground.

As you might guess, this tactic tended to produce more than a little anxiety for friends, family, and supporters watching from the stands. If you didn't know my strategy—and even if you did—it was still hard to watch. For most of the race I'd be well in back of the pacesetters, right on the edge, it would seem, of disaster. Then usually with about a lap or a lap and a half to go, I'd start moving my way up, and the question was always whether I could make up that much ground that quickly. At the very least, it was never boring.

So that was my habit, and over time it became automatic. I almost couldn't burst to the front of a race even if I tried.

For me that strategy worked well enough. I was able to compete on an international level for thirteen years, so it was understandable why I stuck with it. I can look back and accurately call it a "correct" habit for me. I still reflect with amusement on the few times I tried to deviate from that strategy—as an experiment or because I was in a field where I thought I might be better off just taking off—and how I couldn't do it very easily. Even on those occasions when I wasn't racing a strategic steeplechase and was going only for a specific time, I had a difficult time turning off that old impulse of assuming what became known as "my customary position in the rear."

There is a Natural Law that explains why habits are so hard to break. It states:

> **Whenever the mind is presented with opposing beliefs,**
> **it will naturally seek to reduce the conflict.**

If there's a conflict, the mind will naturally first seek to reduce the conflict by going to the most familiar and comfortable route. And that's going to be the one we're used to.

Do you remember back in chapter two when we first discussed the imprinting process? Well, over time these imprints create superhighways of synapses as we constantly commute over them and reaffirm their route.

So it is that when we stand over a golf ball and we're *absolutely determined* to use a new swing, when it comes down to crunch time, we'll still, to our astonishment, use the old swing.

WE CAN CHANGE

When Sam Snead said, "The trouble with most amateurs is they never hit the ball with their practice swing," note that he said *most*. He didn't mean all amateurs, and he couldn't mean that was a condition for life. The only reason that statement has so much universal truth is because it is typically correct. The typical amateur usually plays golf about once a week, if he or she is lucky, and consequently that doesn't offer nearly enough time and energy to create new imprints that will facilitate a smooth transition from old bad swing to new good swing—to a "real" swing that is like the practice swing.

Practice makes perception, in other words. Left alone, our imprints will perpetuate themselves our whole lives, leaving us more and more powerless to change as time goes on. Unless we first create a conflict, by introducing new theoretical beliefs onto our belief windows, and then set to work making that new opposing belief stick, we'll always be a slave to the same old imprints as stamped by the same old beliefs. So the question, and the challenge, becomes: How do we turn the new theoretical belief into reality so that it will drive behavior that will meet our needs over time?

CAN'T EAT JUST ONE

To answer that, let's use an example I think we might all be able to relate to. Let's say our current behavior is to go home after work, when we're tired and hungry, and the first thing we do when we walk in the door is grab a big bowl of potato chips from the pantry and start munching away. Since we can't eat just one, before we know it we're to the bottom of the bowl. Then we recline on the couch, click on the TV, and either watch television or take a nap, or both.

In this experience, what are the positive consequences of our actions? Well, we're not hungry anymore, we're relaxed, and we're getting some rest that feels good. What are the negative consequences? Well, we haven't done much for our body fat, we've raised our cholesterol count, and we won't feel much like moving when we decide it's time to get off the couch. We're sluggish and tired, and later on, when we should go to bed, we're not going to be tired.

Notice that the positive consequences are all immediate and the negative consequences are the ones that don't manifest themselves until later on.

Aware of these negative consequences as we sit there on the couch, feeling full but now somewhat disappointed in ourselves, we say, "I'm not going to do this any more. From now on I'm going to eat only healthy, balanced meals. I'm going to go to the grocery store after work, and I'm going to buy some healthy food. I'll be healthier, I'll have more energy, and I'll reduce my weight." That's our new theo-

retical belief. It's not yet reality. Notice that it's based on positive consequences that will not be immediate and negative consequences (or
what we see as negative consequences) that are more immediate, such
as needing to make that trip to the store after work, the new need to
cook, and the need to delay our hunger until all that is accomplished.
Plus, we've got to give up the potato chips.

That's what we're confronted with the next day after work. We're
tired and hungry again, and we've got two choices. We can go home,
grab the chips, eat the whole bowl, turn on the TV, and doze, or we
can apply our new belief and go to the store, buy healthy food, take it
home, cook it, and eat it.

What are we likeliest to do? Go home and eat the chips and flop on
the couch, of course. Why? Because even though we've produced a
conflict, we'll still naturally gravitate toward solving that conflict
with the easiest and most immediate solution, which is doing what
we've always done. Human nature says seek the immediate solution,
take care of the *now* right now. Human nature takes us to the biggest
path, the most familiar path, the strongest synapse superhighway.
We'll go to the strong imprint, the one with the least resistance, the
familiar one.

OUR TENDENCY IS TO TAKE THE EASY WAY OUT

It's the same with exercise or any of a thousand other examples we
could name. We'll say, "OK, I've got a new belief that says exercise is
good, and I'm going to exercise daily." Then we'll go home and we'll
think, "But I sure love reading the paper, and I don't want to miss the
news on TV." Which of the conflicting behaviors will bring us immediate gratification and which will bring us long-term benefit? Human nature will throw us to immediate gratification every time, and
our *tendency* will always be to take that route. Human nature will
have us reading the paper and watching the news—the things we've
always done and the things that bring us immediate pleasure. The

things that take care of our short-term needs are naturally going to be the most attractive in the short term.

This does not mean, of course, that we are powerless to shuck off the old and get on with the new. It just means that it's not easy, and we shouldn't be surprised when it isn't. Only through dedicated practice and determination can we go from the theoretical to reality by truly creating imprints that result in bigger habits than those we're trying to replace.

That practice and dedication is incumbent upon two other Natural Laws, the first of which says:

A belief is not written on my belief window until it is reflected in my behavior.

Behavior does not lie. Behavior is always an accurate reflection of a belief on a belief window. You can say to yourself or to others, "I believe junk food is bad for me." That's the belief you say is on your belief window. But then you eat a donut. Why are you eating a donut? It might be because you're "going to run it off tonight" or because "it's only one donut." There's a belief you have on your belief window that says eating a donut is acceptable, which in turn says your statement, "I believe junk food is bad for me," is not entirely an adopted belief. No matter how much you insist it is, it can't be. Why? Because you're eating that donut, that's why. That's your behavior, and *behavior does not lie*.

This is true, too, for groups, organizations, and businesses. In my work with corporations I have had a chance to observe many different environments, many varied work atmospheres, and it's not at all difficult to make pretty accurate guesses as to what beliefs are on a company's belief window. As an example, not long ago I was at the Caterpillar company in Chicago doing some work there, and as I drove into their plant the first thing I noticed was a big sign that said QUALITY PEOPLE WORKING TOGETHER TO MAKE QUALITY PRODUCTS. Inside the plant I saw that sign everywhere I turned. There were all kinds of variations on the "Quality" theme, all of them presenting the same basic company belief of quality products being produced by quality people. The interesting thing as I worked with them was that I could see in the Caterpillar employees that they believed that company value. I could see it by their behavior. They acted like quality people. They walked, talked, and acted like quality people. The imprinting, it appeared to me, had taken hold. Their quality behavior reflected that. They truly saw themselves as quality people working together to make quality products.

WE NEED STRUCTURE

Realizing that our behavior conforms to our beliefs, whether we're consciously aware of that or not, only further emphasizes the importance of operating with beliefs that are correct for us. If our behavior reflects incorrect beliefs we need to go about changing our beliefs.

That brings us to the second Natural Law, which says:

Structuring new experiences is the most effective way to create and reinforce new beliefs.

There are three kinds of structured experiences: Actual, Visualized, and Modeling, which are necessary to complete the process of cementing new beliefs onto our belief windows.

Let's examine these structured experiences by using the example of giving a speech. First, let's imagine that we want to create a belief on our belief window that says, "I am good at giving speeches." We know that only with that belief in place can we then drive behavior that will produce good speech-making qualities. Since we have no real history of giving good speeches, this new belief of ours is going to need some help in getting established.

This is where the structuring comes in.

Our initial impulse, of course, would probably be to give a speech.

That would qualify, of course, as an Actual Experience. To do this, we would seek out an opportunity to give a speech; we would conquer any fears we have such as shyness or pronunciation of words so we could physically walk to the podium, and then we would deliver our speech.

By carefully structuring that Actual Experience we would begin the internal imprinting process that, we'd hope, over time would turn us into good speech-givers.

Let's say giving speeches isn't something we naturally feel comfortable about doing. Let's say it downright scares us to even *think* about getting up in front of an audience and giving a speech. We might not even make it to the microphone before we collapse. How can we ever possibly get to the point that we could not only give a speech, but give a good speech?

VISUALIZING PRECEDES THE DEED

The answer is that Actual Experiences are often best preceded by Visualized Experiences.

In the case of the speech, visualizing would entail first seeing the audience in our minds, hearing the audience's applause, hearing the audience's laughter, and hearing ourselves use clear enunciation combined with a confident, powerful delivery. We'd do all this in our minds. We'd imagine conquering all of our fears and concerns.

Visual structuring works because it's just as real to the mind as actual structuring. What we live in our mind we record in our mind. That's what imprinting is. The moment we experience an event vividly in our imagination it is recorded or imprinted as an experience, even though we didn't physically do it.

I personally never ran a race before first living it many times in my mind before I actually competed. I visualized warming up, how fast I was going to run, who else was going to be in the race, and what they would do. I visualized what I would do in case this circumstance or that circumstance came up. I visualized where I wanted to be at the end of each lap. I visualized how I would go over each hurdle. Three of the four times I set American records during my career, I had told my roommate that day in the hotel the lap times I planned to run that night for the record, and on all three occasions I hit those lap times right on. Why? Because I'd already lived it, I'd experienced it, I was already programmed. (The other occasion I set a record was in the 1980 Olympic Trials, and my visualizing was more on making the Olympic team than breaking the record). That's what happens when we visualize. We program our lives. We lay down the imprints that drive us.

As I said at the beginning of this chapter, on those occasions when I did run races for record times, I had to deviate from my usual strategy of running at the back of the pack. If I hadn't visualized extensively before getting to the starting line, I never would have been able to break that old habit of "laying back" long enough to do something different, if only for one night.

We're the Authors

The exciting part of the visualizing process—and this goes for the entire process of achieving our personal best through principle-driven behavior—is that we are the exclusive authors of it. We can make sure that it's enjoyable, rewarding, fulfilling, and satisfying. No matter what we want to accomplish, it gives us the steering wheel to our lives. If we're first successful in our minds, we then put ourselves in position to be successful in our actions.

Let's take a real "far out" example. Let's say we want to overcome a fear we have of skydiving. We're probably not going to go out and skydive a hundred times to conquer that fear. That might not be too advisable. Instead, what we can do is first practice skydiving vividly in our minds over and over, in preparation for that first jump. First we'll learn more about skydiving and all its intricacies. We'll watch videos of people skydiving safely, read books about overcoming fear, talk to people who have actually skydived and survived—and enjoyed it! Then, in our minds, in a relaxed moment, we'll imagine we're up in the plane preparing to jump. We'll feel the heaviness of the pack on our back, the awkwardness of the suit and the straps all around our body. We'll hear the engine of the plane roaring in our ears and the voices of the other jumpers as they shout to be heard above the noise.

We'll see the faces of our cojumpers, and they'll be excited, happy faces, looking forward to what they're about to experience. We're NOT going to imagine faces full of fear and anguish (least of all our own). Now we'll hear and smell and feel the rush of air as the door opens, and the instructor says, "Step out onto the bar and hang on until I say let go." Now we'll see ourselves stepping out and looking down! The wind is strong! The instructor says, "Hang on, hang on . . . NOW! Let go!" And we let go. We feel the air rushing by our ears. Now we find the rip cord and we PULL! Whoosh! All of a sudden, we're going up, up as the parachute opens. This is fun! Now we're floating, sailing through the air safely with the comfort of the parachute above us. We're floating. We're flying. We smell the air. We see the incredible unobstructed 360-degree view that unfolds everywhere in front of our eyes. We feel the straps on our shoulders, our lifeline, and we feel that the straps are secure. We're floating, floating, floating. We're having an incredible experience! Now the ground is approaching rapidly and we're preparing to land. We're going over in our mind how to hit the ground so we won't hurt ourselves. We're going to land perfectly. Now the ground is rushing toward us. It's there. We bend and fold just right. Our knees absorb the shock. We do the roll perfectly as we glide to a stop. The parachute falls gracefully behind us. We stand up and feel exhilarated as we look back up at the sky!

Experiencing a parachute jump like that in our mind prepares us for the actual thing. It makes us *want* to skydive. Such visualizing can be effective in all areas of our lives. We can visualize talking assertively to our supervisor about a project we feel passionately about. We can visualize making an effective sales presentation. We can visualize taking a test for our pilot's license. We can visualize fly fishing on the Madison River in Montana. We can visualize acting in a play. The list goes on and on. Visualizing is limited only by our imagination.

When visualizing helps us realize the establishment of a new belief it becomes an important step along the path of achieving our personal best through principle-driven behavior.

A Terrific Example

One of the best examples of visualizing—and resultant positive consequences—I've ever heard is the Viktor Frankl story as told in his book *Man's Search for Meaning*. Mr. Frankl was a prisoner of war in Germany in World War II, and he tells a horrifying tale of suffering through conditions that were most inhumane. He was stripped of virtually everything physical. He was tortured, starved, and drugged, and made to live in conditions that tested human endurance. In virtually every physical sense, he was a prisoner. Yet he survived. His secret was in recognizing what he had control over and taking advantage of that. He didn't have control over much, but he did have control over his own thoughts. He had control over how he chose to respond to the horrible things done to him. He had control over where he went in his mind. He could see whatever he wanted—in his mind. He could visit wherever he wanted—in his mind. Through effective visualizing, Viktor Frankl survived, and in some ways, actually thrived.

ACTUAL EXPERIENCES

Of course visualizing is only the first step, albeit an extremely important first step. Visualizing has to become a partner with Actual Experiences. Otherwise we'll spend our lives in a fantasy world. By visualizing ourselves behaving in a certain manner we facilitate actually being that way, and every time we behave a certain way we strengthen an imprint, or belief, driving that behavior. So to make a new theoretical belief reality we must structure both Visualized and Actual Experiences in our lives to build new imprints until they are strong enough to overtake the old incorrect beliefs.

As we have discussed, some of our old incorrect beliefs will take a long time to be totally overcome, because we have been "validating" and hence strengthening these incorrect beliefs for many years. Others we can overcome in a matter of days or weeks. It's all going to take effort, but just how much effort can vary greatly.

For example, it took me a year and a half to have my new belief become operative when I switched from being a lawyer to working at Franklin. I didn't change my old belief to my new belief over night. Remember, my old belief was that my self-worth was dependent on how others viewed my profession and that being a lawyer caused others to view me as important. At first, I wasn't so sure about my new profession.

My new theoretical belief was that my self-worth was dependent on how I viewed my profession, and I needed to be in a profession that brought me fulfillment. Only by continually structuring new experiences consistent with my new belief was I able to gradually build the new imprints that over time replaced the old ones and validated the new theoretical belief I had put into place.

First I visualized myself enjoying my work and feeling fulfilled. Then I found a profession compatible with that vision. Then I tried Actual Experiences, actually working in that profession, to see if it would bring about the desired results. For me, it worked, as evidenced by my new behaviors, such as no more hump days or

T.G.I.F.'s. Again, this was no overnight process. It took time to overcome the old belief. Only through these structured experiences was the process able to get to a physical change of jobs. Only after Actual Experiences was I able to change my response from, "I'm an attorney, I work at Franklin," to "I work at Franklin." Only after a good deal of work and effort at structuring new experiences was I able to realize that my new belief was in fact one that would better meet my needs.

MODELING

There's a third technique to help identify and reinforce our new beliefs. It is called Modeling. Modeling is identifying someone who has already implemented the behaviors in his life that we want in any given area of our lives. We then carefully study what our model is doing and has done to be successful and apply the same techniques in our lives.

For example, if we want to be a great real estate agent, we should find a successful agent and follow him around for a week. See what he does to get new clients, how he services his current clients, and how he utilizes past clients. This experience will imprint a picture of success, then from this picture we can identify the experiences (tasks) we need to do to reinforce that imprint.

In other words, we don't have to reinvent the wheel. We can take advantage of someone else's years of experience as a starting point rather than our ending point. We can avoid their mistakes by watching them, consulting with them, or even reading about them. We are thus visualizing our path of success. All that is left for us to do is to implement those behaviors in our lives.

Instant Replay

Key Points

- Changing behavior isn't easy. We need to have a good game plan in place to really change.

- When the mind is presented with opposing beliefs, it will naturally seek to reduce the conflict and try to remain with the most reinforced beliefs.

- By structuring experiences—Actual, Visualized, and Modeling—we can override our mind's desire to maintain the status quo.

- Beliefs aren't truly written on our belief windows until they're reflected in our behavior.

Personal Exercise

- Identify the new beliefs you want to guide specific areas of your life. (See Personal Exercise, chapter ten.)

- Structure experiences that will reinforce the new belief by doing the following:

  (1) Make a list of actual experiences (tasks) you can do starting today. (Focus on what can be done during the next three weeks.)
  (2) Visualize what success looks like in your focus area. (Mentally review that picture every day.)
  (3) Model your life after someone whose behavior reflects your picture of success.
  (4) Select a buddy to whom you can commit to acting on your plan. (If possible select someone pursuing similar goals.)

- Write your structured experiences on task lists in your Day Planner. (Then act on them daily.)

Where Do We Go from Here?

In chapter twelve, I'd like to continue the story I began in chapter three. What happened to me in the Olympic Games of 1984 and, most important, how I reacted to what happened illustrates the importance of applying those two words, "over time," to our beliefs.

Personal Peace

If I hadn't changed my beliefs, what happened in
the Los Angeles Olympic Games would still haunt me
today.

The hardest part was the waiting.

It was a warm, almost muggy, Los Angeles twilight as I stretched
my leg muscles on the warmup track adjacent to the Los Angeles
Memorial Coliseum. In an hour I would compete in the steeplechase
final of the 1984 Los Angeles Olympic Games. It was an event I had
been waiting for for most of the past decade, ever since I decided not
to quit the track team at BYU in January of 1976, fueled by my new
beliefs.

I was thirty years old, and this wasn't my first Olympic experience.
My first Olympic Games had been in Montreal in 1976, where I
roomed with Bruce Jenner, who set a world record in the de-
cathlon—thanks in no small part, I would forever believe, to my
Jethro Tull collection of eight-track tapes, which Jenner listened to
faithfully each night in preparation for the next day's competition.

I finished tenth in the Montreal Olympics and was the top placing
American in my race. All in all a heady experience for a guy no one
had heard anything about; a guy who needed to wear a "Hello, my
name is . . ." tag wherever he went. My time of 8:23.9 in the Montreal
final meant I had lowered my personal best time by just over one
minute in less than seven months—and was within seven-tenths of a
second of the fastest steeplechase ever run by an American. If any-

body needed more encouragement to keep running, if anybody needed extra motivation to see what was over the next hill, well, it wasn't me.

I was well aware of where I stood in the international scheme of things, and that there were some intriguing possibilities on the horizon, but I was determined to keep that competitiveness in check. I wanted to be sure I continued to subscribe to my new belief of concentrating on my own effort and not on the effort of others. To that end, I continued to be something of a loner on the workout track, a maverick who kept his head down, his eyes only on his own stop watch. I had seen what happened when I looked at others and not at myself.

Thanks, in part, to excellent coaching along the way—first from Sherald James at BYU and then from Bill Bowerman, the head coach at the University of Oregon and a pioneer at Nike, who took me under his wing—and blessed, too, with reasonably good health, I thrived on the international circuit. The post-Montreal days were good ones for me. I set a new American record; won national championships in 1978, 1979, and 1980; and won several world-class races, including the Pan American Games in 1979 and the big pre-Olympic meet in Russia called Spartakaide. By the time I made my second United States Olympic Team in 1980 I was ranked number four in the world, and my winning time in the United States Olympic Trials was the fastest that year anywhere in the world.

At that point, my Olympic hopes, along with every other member of the U.S. team, were blindsided by political unrest. Because those 1980 games were to be held in Moscow, the capital of the Soviet Union, and because the Soviets invaded Afghanistan in January of 1980, our president, Jimmy Carter, elected to protest that invasion by pulling the U.S. team out of the Moscow Games.

It was a tough pill to swallow, I'll be the first to admit. In the world of track and field, the Olympics are the litmus test of your career, and each career doesn't get many such litmus tests. I was twenty-six years old in 1980 and dreamed of wearing an Olympic medal around my neck, perhaps even a gold medal, and it was no small disappointment to get over the dashing of that chance, especially since I could see no correlation between world politics and me running a steeplechase race in a sports gathering dedicated to peace and the brotherhood of man.

Still, as Moscow came and went, I ran on. I managed to graduate from law school at the University of Oregon and began my practice as an attorney, but it was running that remained my passion, and the Olympic Games of 1984 became my new ideal, my lighthouse on the shore. Surely we wouldn't boycott an Olympics we would host. To that end I successfully won four more consecutive national titles and lowered the American record again. In 1981 and 1982 I was the number one ranked steeplechaser in the world, and in 1983 I was ranked number two. In Los Angeles, competing on my home turf, so to speak, I would be the favorite even if I didn't want to be.

That favored status was only increased when the Soviet Bloc countries announced they would not be coming to Los Angeles. The way they saw it, one boycott deserved another. That meant a number of good steeplechasers, including Boguslaw Maminski of Poland, ranked number three in the world, would not be in the field.

When Patriz Ilg of West Germany, the man who was ranked number one in the world in 1983, pulled out of the Olympics because of tonsilitis, the way to the gold medal was as prepared for Henry Marsh as it could be. I couldn't argue with that. A lot of excellent runners would still be competing, of course, but there was no question that I would be the favorite. I knew it and so did everyone else who had a passing knowledge of my event.

To that end I became something of a celebrity, or at least as much of a celebrity as a person can become who participates in an event he first has to explain. The American TV networks all did profiles on who I was, where I'd come from, that kind of thing. Camera crews would fly into Salt Lake City and drive to our home in Bountiful, an adjoining suburb, where I would trace my history the best I could and try to be colorful. I cut back on my workload at the law firm, to about

50 percent, so I could fit in all the distractions and still leave room for quality workouts. The last thing I wanted to do was neglect my training. Every few weeks during the early part of 1984 I would fly to Los Angeles and meet Coach Bowerman, who would put me through simulated racing conditions in the Olympic climate. If we could help it, the L.A. smog was not going to be foreign to me or my lungs.

I should add that I thoroughly enjoyed all of it. I enjoyed running the steeplechase, and I enjoyed the atmosphere of the Olympic Games. I enjoyed the opportunities that were presented, I enjoyed being number one, and I enjoyed getting the chance to be a part of the Olympic Games again. I enjoyed the contract I signed with Nike. I enjoyed the endorsement deals that were lining up. These were dreams come true, goals accomplished, and I can honestly say I was thrilled with the process.

But I wasn't thrilled when I got sick.

The doctors told me it was a virus. They didn't know for sure which virus, but they knew for certain that not only was it a virus, it was a powerful virus.

If I could have personally chosen the worst possible time to hear this news, it would have been precisely when I heard it. It was in late June of 1984, just a few days after the U.S. Track and Field Olympic Trials had been held at the Los Angeles Coliseum, soon to be the site of the Olympic Games. The Trials, which constituted the 1984 U.S. championships, had gone as well as I'd hoped. I ran last most of the race, and then used a healthy kick to win comfortably. It was my seventh straight national championship, and that pleased me; it extended a string of unbeaten races that sretched back almost a full year.

It looked like everything was coming together. If I was a betting man, I'd have bet on myself. For the past six months I had paid close attention to my diet and tried to rest as much as possible, and, as I said, I cut down on my legal practice—all in concert with my Olympic game plan.

Maybe I inadvertently overworked getting ready for the U.S. Trials, or maybe I was just unlucky. I don't know. But I do know that a week after the Trials and five weeks before the start of the Olympic Games in Los Angeles, I was flat in bed, felled by a bug of mysterious origin.

I rested and then tried to rest some more. Talk about your conflicts, I had a classic dilemma on my hands. On the one hand I knew the very best way to beat a virus was to rest. On the other hand I knew the very best way to lose an Olympic medal was to rest.

I tried to compromise.

I'd take just so much of my bed, and then I'd get up and work out. I couldn't help myself. Above all, a runner has to run. I remember one day at home in Bountiful when I got out of bed after a full day of taking it easy and then got on the treadmill and ran ten miles at my normal six minute-per-mile training pace.

After that I reached for my training log, quickly scribbled, "Not feeling 100 percent," and collapsed back into bed. I was a pathetic sight.

I couldn't shake this thing, whatever it was, and instinctively I knew it. It had its own course to run, that virus, and it was running it.

I went to Eugene, Oregon, for a pre-Olympic race and shouldn't have. I lost for the first time in nearly a year and for the first time ever to my American teammate, Brian Diemer, who was trying to work up a good dose of confidence heading into the L.A. games. At least I was helping somebody's preparation.

I flew to Los Angeles for the first day of the Olympics, where I marched with the United States team in the spectacular opening ceremonies held in the coliseum. I enjoyed the spectacle as President Ronald Reagan opened the games of the Twenty-third Olympiad, and more than 90,000 spectators cheered the world's Olympians as they marched onto the track. By many accounts, those L.A. games turned out to be among the best ever staged, and no one could argue that they weren't launched in grand style. But as for me, I know I'd have enjoyed the festivities more if it hadn't been for the dizzy light-headed feeling.

Determined to rest and relax, I didn't stay in the Olympic Village with the rest of the athletes. I checked into the home of a family friend in Beverly Hills, where I reasoned that I could get plenty of down time with a minimum of distractions. I didn't think it would help my chances any if I spent my days in the Olympic Village. For one thing, I wouldn't get much rest amid all the commotion in the village. For another, the less my opponents knew about my condition, the better. I was determined to be a recluse.

It did help. Luckily, the steeplechase wasn't first on the Olympic program. I had more than a week after the opening ceremonies before my first qualifying heat was scheduled, another day before my second qualifying heat (providing I survived the first one), and a day between that heat and the final, to be held on the second to last day of the games.

The virus and the Olympic final were playing a game of chicken, and I was coming along for the ride.

I made it out of the first heat, placing fourth among the six finalists who moved on to the semifinals. In the semis I again weathered the crowd, again finishing fourth in a race that qualified six into the finals. Virus or no virus, I would be one of twelve runners who, in the early evening of August 10, 1984, would compete in the Olympic final, racing for the three medals at the finish line.

All of which brought me to the coliseum's warmup track an hour before race time, where as I stretched, I tried to get a grip on everything I was feeling.

As I listened to the hum of 90,000 voices inside the stadium and as I tried to coax a hamstring to go to new lengths, I gave myself a pregame talk. What I said to myself was that I was about to compete in a race that, for whatever reasons, would be very important to me. It was what I had set my sights on, what I had trained for, what I had designated as significant for most of my adult life—and since that was the case, when I got inside the stadium and they finally fired the gun that sent us off, I needed to make certain I didn't hold anything back.

I needed to give it all I had. That was my pep talk. Everything. Virus or no virus, alibi or no alibi, that's what I needed to do. If that got me the gold medal, fantastic! If it got me last place, well that would be all right, too. The important thing was that after the race was over I could look myself in the mirror and be able to say in the affirmative that I gave it my all.

That done, I walked into the coliseum. I had no idea what to expect. Probably the last thing I expected was to see Mary Decker-Slaney being carried off the track in the arms of her husband, Richard Slaney.

Mary Decker, as she had been known throughout her illustrious running career, was a close friend as well as an Olympic teammate. We ran for the same club, Athletics West, and our careers had connected in many ways. She was a multiple-time national champion and had won many major middle-distance races all around the world. In 1983 she won the world championship at 3,000 meters and was the favorite at that distance in Los Angeles as well. The only trophy not on her shelf was an Olympic medal—Mary, too, had been a casualty of the 1980 Moscow boycott—and L.A.'s home turf was seen as her place of redemption. In many ways, our stories paralleled each other. Both of us came to the games of 1984 with high hopes and high expectations—and a good deal of attention. Along with the sprinter and long jumper, Carl Lewis, we were America's track-and-field odds-on favorites in 1984.

And now here was Mary, lying limply in the arms of her husband as he carried her to medical attendants who were waiting at the side of the track. Out on the track I noticed that the women's 3,000-meter race was still going on. I soon learned that there had been a collision just beyond the halfway point of the race. Mary and Zola Budd, a South African running for Great Britain, had collided, and Mary had crashed to the track, unable to continue the race. A shaken Budd ran on but, although she was leading at the time of the collision, faded to seventh place. Maricica Puica of Romania crossed the finish line first to claim the gold medal—not far from where Mary, in an obvious state of physical and mental anguish, was unsuccessfully trying to choke back the tears.

My heart went out to my friend and teammate. I knew how she felt and how painful that moment was for her. She did not deserve this. An already sober evening had just turned even more sober. With that in mind, I reported to the starting line for the beginning of the Olympic final in the men's 3,000-meter steeplechase. I hoped it wasn't an omen.

I was off with the gun, more or less. I assumed my customary position in the rear and let my head clear. It felt good to be running. It felt good to have the wait over. It felt good to finally be *doing this*. There were some good runners in the field but I was comforted by the fact that none had personal-best times as low as mine—a statistic by now well known to anyone listening to television or reading the newspapers. If I just had the stamina . . .

As the race wore on it became obvious to me, from my backseat position, that two Kenyans with the same first name, Julius Korir and Julius Kariuki, were going to have to be dealt with. Neither of the Juliuses had an international reputation—as was often the case with talented Kenyans who tended to materialize at the Olympic Games—but I could tell by the way they were running that they had the talent to be in it for the long haul. The same went for Joseph Mahmoud, a proven commodity from France who was ranked fifth in the world, and of course for my teammate Diemer. I kept them all in sight.

With a lap to go I was right where I wanted to be and feeling OK so far. I was running on adrenaline, and so far, so good. I just hoped I wouldn't be too weakened for the stretch run, when my reserve of stamina would really be needed.

I moved from seventh to fifth. Then, on the back straightaway I passed, in order, Mahmoud, Diemer, and Kariuki. I was at the shoulder of the second Kenyan, Korir, as Al Michaels, the ABC commentator broadcasting the race, said, "And here comes Marsh!" Three hundred yards, one water jump, and one final barrier stood between this moment and the Olympic gold medal.

Much as I wanted to make Michaels look good, I never did get past Korir. I came to his shoulder, maybe six inches from taking the lead, but he held me off and stayed in front; by the water jump at the last corner he had extended his lead to several yards. He went over the water first, then me. Mahmoud and Diemer soon followed, with Kariuki fading.

Less than one hundred meters to go, it became obvious that Korir was going to be one tough Kenyan to catch. Meanwhile, there's the Frenchman and my American teammate to worry about. At the final barrier Mahmoud surged past me. He wasn't going to be easy to catch either. Up ahead, Korir was breaking the tape for the win and the gold medal, and Mahmoud was closing fast to take the silver. The bronze medal would go to one of two Americans—me or the one closing quickly behind me.

My teammate passed me just before we crossed the line. Brian Diemer beat me out for the bronze medal by nineteen-hundredths of a second. Less than two feet.

Fourth place was mine. As I said then and still say, "Fourth place, the worst possible finish. You don't get a medal, and you still have to go through drug-testing."

Only for me the drug-testing had to wait. As soon as I crossed the thin white line that said "you can stop now," I collapsed onto the track and fell quite unconscious. I have watched the videotape of that race many times since and still find it curious to view myself going through something I have no memory of. As the other runners finished, several stooped down to see if I was all right, looking curiously at this crumpled figure who only moments before had been ahead of them on the back straightaway, going for broke.

Within moments an ambulance drove onto the track, and a team of paramedics lifted me onto a stretcher and into the back of the ambulance, which transported me to the small infirmary that adjoins the coliseum. The crowd didn't know what was wrong with me and, at that moment, neither did I.

As it turned out, nothing was wrong except I had run out of fuel, gas, combustion, whatever you want to call it. My body had taken over and simply shut down. It wasn't going an inch farther. It was as simple as that. About thirty minutes later I regained consciousness in the infirmary and swung my feet off the cot and onto the floor. I walked to the parking lot and drove myself home.

The next day, and for several days after that, the commotion hit. To this day I'm amazed at the compassion and outpouring of empathy that took place. I got telegrams and cards and letters from all around the country, commiserating with my bad turn of luck. At the track the next night I was personally inundated by well-meaning supporters who shook their heads and said, "too bad," and "that must be devastating."

Now don't get me wrong. I appreciated then, and still do, the genuine affection and empathy that was displayed. Many people showed kindness. Perfect strangers expressed their sympathy. But no sooner was the 1984 Olympic final over, than I honestly felt none of the devastation and gut-wrenching defeat many people expected I would— and that many of them were feeling.

I was disappointed, to be sure. I don't think I'll ever forget the frustration I felt that August night in the summer of 1984. I didn't stop being human. I wanted that gold medal as much as anyone (I also wouldn't have minded the $40,000 bonus Nike, one of my sponsors, was offering if I won it).

But I wasn't kidding when I said I could live with what happened. I wasn't kidding when I said it was disappointing, to be sure, but it was hardly devastating. In my own mind, it was just the opposite. As far as I was concerned, I had won. The reason was because I had satisfied my own game plan, my own belief. Winning the gold medal wasn't my game plan. Giving it all I had was my game plan. I did that. I could not argue with myself that I had given it everything I had when I collapsed unconscious just beyond the finish line.

The same belief that enabled me to rejoin my college track team after I quit some eight years before was anchored even more securely on my belief window by the time the Olympic Games of 1984 came along. For me, that turned out to be a good thing. A very good thing.

Just why I was lucky enough to stumble—and I did stumble—upon the concept of principle-driven behavior when I was twenty-one years old I'm not sure. But I count it as one of the most significant stumbles of my life. Without a correct belief on my belief window in Los Angeles I could have been saddled with a devastation that would have been enormous. I have seen other athletes in similar situations, and I know it can be debilitating if you're not careful.

Certainly I have often reflected on the coincidence surrounding my experience in Los Angeles and the experience of my friend and teammate, Mary Decker-Slaney. Both of us had to deal with an Olympic experience that didn't conclude as we'd hoped for—a medal hanging from our necks as the national anthem was played and the stars and stripes raised up the flagpole. That was tough for a couple of veteran performers and prerace favorites. Mary's reaction was different from mine. Her grief was more profound, her outrage more pronounced, for what I think are very understandable reasons. I'm sure her belief window reflected a belief that said you were successful when you beat other people—just as mine once had. That being the case, when you don't beat other people your needs are going to be severely threatened, and that's difficult to deal with. Mary carried that Los Angeles "defeat" with her for a long time. It affected how she raced in the future. It affected her affection for running. All because of the beliefs on her belief window. Both of us could say life hadn't been fair because of external obstacles—for me the virus and for her the runner who tripped her up—but how we dealt with that realization, how we chose to behave in response, depended on the beliefs that drove us. We were bound to them.

There was a remarkable moment in Atlanta during the 1996 Summer Olympics with Mary Decker-Slaney twelve years after her mishap with Zola Budd. Through years of injuries Mary kept at it.

As in 1984, Mary did not make it to the medal stand; in fact, in 1996 she was eliminated in a preliminary round. However, her response to not winning a medal was very different. In 1996 she was satisfied with the opportunity to be able to compete in the Olympics at what was considered an "old age." Her belief and driving force was no longer centered around winning. It was now based on being able to compete and give it her best shot.

It's our beliefs that determine how we're going to behave in any situation; it's our beliefs that allow us to be in control of our lives or out of control. Our beliefs determine if life's whims are going to decide when and where we land, or if we'll decide that ourselves. Applying correct beliefs and behaving accordingly is the key to a healthy, happy life. I am convinced of that. I still wish I had a gold medal hanging from my fireplace mantel. But I know I can live, and I know I can still feel self-worth, without it.

Instant Replay

Key Points

- Having a correct belief in place allowed me to appreciate my Olympic experience even without a gold medal—or any medal for that matter—draped around my neck.

- Our success is measured by personal beliefs, not by anybody else's standards or beliefs.

Personal Exercise

- Identify examples in your life where you had a "correct belief" which was different from others around you (boss, spouse, coworker, child, neighbor, client).

- Identify examples in your life where you judged other people by your beliefs when your beliefs were not correct for those people.

Where Do We Go from Here?

In chapter thirteen, we'll go through a step-by-step process for employing new personal beliefs.

Practical Application

So you really want to change a belief! Here's how.

By now we've established this core truth: The quality of our lives is going to be no better, and no worse, than the strength of our beliefs.

Correct beliefs will drive behavior that will produce results that will satisfy our needs over time.

Incorrect beliefs will drive behavior that will produce results that will not satisfy our needs over time.

End of discussion.

When we accept this core truth, our search for happiness, peace, and fulfillment will focus only on beliefs, our own beliefs. No matter how much money we might have or how many cars, toys, or houses; no matter how often our picture is in the paper or how many times we've visited the White House; no matter where we went to college, where we live, who we know, or where we work: All of these are ineffective at meeting our needs over time if our beliefs are incorrect.

Think about people you know, people you've studied, people you see on television, in the movies, or in sporting events. Look at their lives. Do some appear happy? Do some appear tormented? Does it seem to matter whether they're rich or poor, famous or anonymous, short or tall, white or brown?

The answer, of course, is no. It doesn't seem to matter. You can take two people with nearly identical circumstances, and one can be quite content with life and the other in constant conflict with it. What's the difference? What's the answer to this mystery?

CORRECT MEANS CONTENTED

The answer is beliefs. If you knew what their beliefs were, it wouldn't be a mystery at all. The contented person is driven by beliefs that are correct for him or her. The person with conflict is driven by beliefs that are incorrect for him or her.

Whether we realize it consciously or not (and many times we do not), it's our correct beliefs that are our most valuable possession. They're far more valuable than wealth, fame, youth, good looks, a good curve ball, or winning the lottery.

None of these assets—valuable though they might be—can do what correct beliefs do. Correct beliefs are what drive us to behave in a way that helps us to consistently meet our needs—all four of them—over time. Our needs to live, to love, to have variety, and to have self-worth are all satisfied when we have correct beliefs in place. What could be more valuable than that? It's our correct beliefs that can help us accept life on all its terms, both the fair and the unfair. It's our correct beliefs that help us flow with the things we can't control, instead of fighting upstream against them. It's our correct beliefs that help us understand those things we can control and use them to our advantage.

AFFORDABLE TO ALL

The good news is that, despite the fact that you couldn't put a price on their value, creating correct beliefs is something we all can do, regardless of our circumstances. We can all "afford" them. Correct beliefs don't cost anything to acquire, at least not in terms of cash up front. They don't weigh anything. They're easy to carry. They do not discriminate. There's no age limit, no race limits, no favoritism, no quotas, and no politics involved. And the supply is unlimited. You can't have too many.

One thing correct beliefs don't have is a written owner's manual. They don't come with one. They don't come with instructions on how to put them together, how to maintain them, and how to fix them. They're not clearly marked in English so we can identify the correct ones from the incorrect ones.

In our effort to better facilitate change through correct beliefs, there's nothing to stop us from putting together an owner's manual on our own.

Over the years, I've become a proponent of creating correct beliefs *before* the pain makes us do it. We've discussed the billions of dollars and tens of millions of annual prescriptions to treat the "diseases of choice" that bring untold amounts of pain, suffering, low self-esteem, lost productivity, and lifelong regrets. We have control over the beliefs that drive these behaviors and responses. I've formulated a Five Step plan to help us better visualize and implement that control.

THE FIVE STEP PLAN

The Five Step plan is simply something tangible we can look at to help us better visualize reality. It can be very effective as an aid when you've come to the conclusion that beliefs *are* important, and you'd like to have a systematic process to follow to implement the beliefs that will drive your peak performance.

These are the five steps:

1. Identify a stressor (person, situation, event, challenge) in your life and the associated habitual emotional responses to that stressor.
2. Identify the incorrect belief and need(s) the stressor threatens by asking, "Why does the stressor make you respond with that emotion?" Follow that by asking, "So what, why is that a threat to you?"

209

3. Identify your life's experiences that created and validated the incorrect belief in the first place.
4. Identify a theoretical new correct belief or "Why Not" to replace the incorrect belief.
5. Structure experiences (Actual, Visualized, and Modeling) to sufficiently imprint the new correct belief so it becomes strong enough to replace the old incorrect belief.

You'll find that the Five Step plan has universal applicability. It can be used in all facets of life, at home, at work, at play, within interpersonal relationships, anywhere and everywhere. Simply plug in the stressor of your choice in step one and proceed from there.

Remember, our definition of "stressor" as discussed in chapter five is that it's an obstacle; it's something we see that gets in the way of us getting what we want. It's stressors that cause us unrest, anxiety, distress, pain—in a word, stress—as we respond to the *perception* of the threats. Stressors are what we perceive as obstacles getting in the way of where we'd like to go and achieving what we want. In turn, it's our response that creates the undesirable symptoms (discussed in chapter five).

IDENTIFY STRESSORS

Remember, too, that when we choose to deal with these symptoms or stressors we'll often turn to quick-fix remedies in an attempt to eliminate the discomfort we're feeling. These remedies range from over-the-counter drugs to prescription drugs, from oversleeping to obsessive shopping. It's a big list, and it can lead to big addictions—addictions that can keep us in the same stressful ruts indefinitely.

So it's important to first identify our stressor. Once we've successfully done that, we're ready to move on with the Five Step plan and the implementation of a new correct belief on our personal belief window.

For our purposes here, let's use a hypothetical workplace stressor and run it through the Five Step plan to see how it works. There are many stressors we could choose, but for the purposes of this example, let's use "deadlines."

Deadlines are a common stressor. Deadlines cause a lot of people a lot of grief. From a practical standpoint, deadlines are very important. Without an identifiable completion time, most projects would lack focus and organization. Things just wouldn't get done. We all need deadlines. I know some writers, for instance, who say they'd never get anything written if they didn't have a deadline compelling them to stop dreaming and start writing.

I also know people for whom deadlines aren't a stressor at all. I think that's important to note. "Deadline" isn't necessarily a bad word. Deadlines don't stress everyone. Some people are inspired and intrigued by deadlines. Their perception of them is 100 percent positive. They don't do their best work until a deadline is staring them in the face. This includes many of history's greatest athletes. For example, Joe Montana, the longtime San Francisco 49er, isn't known as arguably the greatest quarterback of all time simply because of his statistics. There are, in fact, quarterbacks who have thrown for many more yards and more touchdowns than he did in his career. But Joe Montana loved a deadline. Give him the ball with just a minute or two left on the clock and a game to be won or lost, and he was at his absolute best. For him, "deadline" was music to his ears. It meant performance. The belief he had on his belief window about deadlines was absolutely correct for him. Just ask all those teams he sent home empty-handed at the end of the Super Bowls.

For the purposes of our Five Step plan, we're going to say that "deadline" isn't inspiring for you at all. It's a bad word with an even nastier connotation. You perceive deadlines as nothing less than necessary evils that exist to haunt you and make your life miserable. For you, deadlines produce anxiety and irritability, increased blood pressure, racing pulse—you have a strong desire to dive under the covers and go to sleep until it's all over.

You're afraid of deadlines. You're petrified of deadlines.

They're your stressor. Maybe you use drugs to deal with the pain they cause you, either over-the-counter drugs or perhaps something your doctor gives you. Maybe you have high blood pressure as the result of deadlines, and you can feel an ulcer coming on. Maybe there are other addictions in your life that are the result of your aversion to deadlines—addictions that circumvent the overall quality of your work and life.

Remember, this is just a hypothetical example. We're just imagining here. Hopefully, it's close enough to reality so you can relate to this exercise.

You've decided you've had enough pain associated with facing deadlines. You're tired of the anger, frustration, anxiety, and depression. You don't want to feel that way anymore. You don't want to take the drugs to try to deal with it. You don't want to feel like running away. You don't want the doctor to take your blood pressure and whistle. You want to find a new correct belief that won't make you feel so helpless and out of control.

So, having identified your stressor and the habitual negative emotional responses that it drives, you go to step two. You want to identify the incorrect belief and the need being threatened.

Begin by Asking Why

First you ask, "Why?"

"Why do deadlines cause frustration, anxiety?"

Let's say your first response as you engage in this self-talk is "Deadlines make me anxious because I'll look bad or incompetent if I miss them."

Then you ask, "So what?" Why is it threatening to me if I look incompetent?

You answer, "My boss will give me a bad review and I could lose my job." (Hence the need being threatened is the need to live, and the incorrect belief is "my livelihood is dependent on meeting my boss's deadlines.")

Notice every answer is a belief.

So we continue talking to ourselves.

"Why will I lose my job?"

"Because that's what happens when the boss isn't happy."

"But have I ever lost a job because I missed a deadline?"

"Well, no."

"Have I ever even seen *someone else lose a job because of a missed deadline?"*

"Not for just missing one."

"Come to think of it, have I ever even missed a deadline?"

"Nope."

"So why do I loathe deadlines?"

"Good question."

THE THIRD STEP: THIRD GRADE

So you think deeper, and as you think deeper you move into step three of our Five Step plan. You examine your life's experiences. You go back to to the roots of where you got your beliefs. You go to your imprints. What do you find there? Well, for the sake of this example, let's say you go back to, of course, the ever popular third grade.

It was in the third grade (or thereabouts) that you learned, for the first time, that if you didn't turn your assignment in on time there was a price to pay. Maybe you got a failing grade. Maybe you got a lecture. Maybe you got rapped on the knuckles by the teacher.

Now you realize that you loathe deadlines because you're still being driven by the belief you put on your belief window way back then. You had a painful experience, and it left an imprint that's turned into a superhighway by the time you're an adult.

As a consequence, you're still behaving as if you're in third grade. You got your belief in school. (Schools are no doubt the largest factory of imprints there is; where else do we have so many values and consequences imprinted on our minds?) Ever since, that belief has driven your behavior. It's *still* driving you all these years later, determining your response and your behavior today. As is often the case, through your penetrating "why?" questions you've discovered that your perception is a lot worse than the reality.

Some of you may be saying that "My livelihood is dependent on meeting my boss's deadlines" is a correct belief. But why isn't it? Remember the Natural Law that says, "When my self-worth is dependent on something external I will not meet my needs over time"? The same law applies for all of our needs. Whenever we base any need on something external it will drive negative behaviors and responses over time. Therefore we just learn to internalize our needs to find correct beliefs.

INTERNAL IS THE KEY

Now you're ready to implement step four. George Bernard Shaw said, "You see things as they are and ask, why? I dream things that never were and ask, why not?" That quote summarizes step four. Let's go back to our example. Now you want to identify a theoretical new belief or "why not" about deadlines that bases meeting your need to live on something over which you have control. It must be a belief that will drive behavior that will produce results that will satisfy your need to live. You'll ask, "Can I base my need to live on something over which I have control?" The answer is yes. You can control how you perform in meeting deadlines even if you don't have control over the deadline. You can do that by concentrating on your own performance. Remember, your productivity will always go up when you focus on the things over which you have control.

In theory, then, you begin thinking about what new belief would eliminate "deadlines" as a stressor? Why not, "Deadlines are there to help me do my job, and I'll do all I can to meet them. Without them, I wouldn't have the proper focus. Deadlines are helpful. They're a part of the best job I have available to me to make the most out of my life. They enhance my performance."

Your theoretical new belief turns a deadline into an asset, a necessary part of your life. You're not going to look at deadlines any more worrying what will happen if you don't meet them; you're going to focus on how to reach your peak performance and on what will happen when you *do* meet them.

As we discussed in chapter three, note that the stressor, or obstacle, did not change. The only thing that changed was your perception of it. Armed with this new perception, your anxiety, your irritability, and all the rest of those negative responses—the essence of what we call stress—are eliminated.

But all this is still in theory for the moment. In step four all you've come up with is what you think the new belief ought to be.

In step five, you will structure experiences that will make the new belief strong enough so it is capable of replacing the old one.

You Can Control Yourself

This is where the work comes in. This is where you have to meet head-on your body's predisposition to stay the same, to not rock the boat, to not change. Knowing your biggest opponent is in fact yourself gives you an edge—That is, if you'll take it. And what's the edge? The fact that you have control over yourself, that's what. Control is important. *Control what you can, and can the rest.* If we've built up addictions long enough or gotten especially good at masking the pain, we may think we can't control ourselves, and we may prove to be a formidable opponent for a time, but a beatable opponent nonetheless. If we're willing to put new beliefs on our belief windows, and give them a chance, we can eventually prevail.

In the case of your old (and powerful) incorrect "deadlines" belief vs. your new (and weak) correct "deadlines" belief, you decide to structure enough experiences so you will be able to slowly but surely turn the tables. First, you decide you want somehow to visualize the luxury you'd feel when you'd not only met your deadlines, but met them with time to spare so you'd have plenty of time to either take care of any emergencies at the last minute or enjoy the indulgence of having a little extra time on your hands. Remember, you have never missed a deadline—the perception in this case is much worse than the reality. You do all this in your mind, and it feels good!

After that, you decide you want to make sure that in your upcoming assignments over, say, the next six months you want to be especially careful to exercise discipline to finish well before you need to. You want to make sure you're well organized, and you put forth your very best effort. Remember, your goal is to create a new belief about deadlines, one that drives behavior that produces results that meet your needs. You understand that to establish that belief, you're going to have to have patience, especially at the beginning. The imprint you're seeking will not be made overnight or after just one test.

You realize, too, that structuring experiences means Modeling. Find someone whose work is well respected, who consistently meets deadlines. Observe them, get to know them. Find out what they do to be successful. What are their habits, techniques, routines? Then implement what you see and learn from them in your daily routine.

After you've taken "deadlines" through the Five Step plan, notice that nothing has changed about deadlines. They're still there, impassive as ever, intangible finish lines; nothing more, nothing less. You've been diligent and patient, and you've allowed yourself to make mistakes along the way, with the end result that you have a whole new outlook on deadlines. Now you see them not only as essential, but you look forward to them. You're glad you have them. You're better at what you do because of them. They elicit productive behavior from you. They enhance your career.

A healthy feeling of self-worth is the result, and your need is taken care of.

You put your belief through the Five Step plan, and it worked!

DEAL WITH IT

It would be helpful for all of us if we'd take the time to identify all of the stressors in our lives, and then systematically put each of them through the Five Step plan. That would be one way we could understand which ones are posing as obstacles to us and why—and what we're going to do about them.

I know a man who is required to move regularly with his company. It's a good company, it has helped him progress quickly in his career, it more than meets the financial needs of his family, and the future looks bright.

This is a good job, and this man loves it dearly. He's not about to give it up. The line is deep and long waiting for jobs like his. He knows he's lucky to have it.

But he has a problem. Every time he has to move he thinks the world is coming to an end. He hates moving. He detests moving. Moving puts him in a foul mood. And yet, it's part of his job. He knows he will periodically be required to move to another part of the country.

I asked him once just why he hates moving so much, and he gave the rote answers. It's disruptive. The kids have to change schools. His wife has to make new friends. They have to sell the old house and buy a new house.

Moving is obviously a stressor for this man. Every three or four years, it causes him all sorts of unrest and pain.

I don't know him well enough to know exactly where his belief about "moving" was developed, but I know from his behavior that it's not, for him, a correct belief. How do I know that? Well, first I know that it's his belief that drives his behavior, and I know by observing his behavior that it's producing results that don't meet his needs. Just the thought of moving can ruin his day. If his needs are not being met, that, by definition, means an incorrect belief. A correct one wouldn't have him in conflict. If he had a correct belief on his belief window, he wouldn't be in stress every time he moves.

If I were in his shoes, I'd want to change my belief about moving if I could. To do that, I'd employ the Five Step plan.

First, I'd identify my stressor (moving) and the associated negative habitual emotional response (anxiety and anger).

Second, I'd ask "Why?" and "So what?" Through these questions I'd determine why I hated moving so much.

Third, I'd get in touch with my life experiences that established my belief about moving—a belief that, through my behavior, says that moving is disruptive and painful. Maybe I'd find I had parents who moved a lot, and I had some bad experiences because of it; maybe that's where my pain comes from. Maybe I'd find I'd constantly heard others in the company complain about moving, and that left a major imprint on me.

Whatever I'd find, it would uncover why I had an incorrect belief about moving.

Fourth, I'd identify a theoretical new belief about moving—something like: "Moving is good for my career. If I don't move, I won't be successful, and my family won't prosper." In other words, moving is part of the path I choose to take, which will maximize my circumstances.

Finally, for the fifth and final step, I'd structure Actual, Visualized, and Modeling experiences that would help me look at moving as a positive experience, not a negative one. Perhaps I'd arrange to coordinate a family vacation around the next move so it would be something to look forward to instead of more drudgery. I'd visualize the benefits I receive from my job that outweigh any negatives associated with moving. I'd look at the lives of people I want to emulate who used moving as an integral part of their success.

FOR OUR OWN BEST INTEREST

Again, I wouldn't touch the stressor, I wouldn't change it one bit. The fact is, I *couldn't* change it. Moving would still entail all that it ever entailed. I wouldn't make a value judgment about moving for the whole world. But I most certainly would change my perception about moving. For me it wouldn't be unpleasant any more. If I'm going to do it in my job and know I'm going to do it, and if the reasons I'm going to do it are in my best interest, then it's only for my own good that I establish a belief on my belief window that says moving is good.

Only then will I drive behavior that produces results that meet my needs over time.

It's important to realize, too, that stressors are not universal. One person's stressor may be another person's motivator. One person may naturally crave having a deadline. It makes him or her work better while another person goes pale at the mere thought of a deadline. One person may covet speaking in front of a large group while the next person may fear that more than just about anything in the world.

Remember, stress is a response to a perception. If we perceive of something as a threat, then it becomes our stressor. The less stressors, the better.

In business, stressors can occur on a companywide level as well. They need to be addressed just the same as individual stressors. The Five Step plan is just as applicable.

I knew an import company that for years had enjoyed a monopoly because no one else carried its main product. Then one year a rival company entered the arena. It, too, imported the same product. Suddenly, a race was on. Competition had entered the picture.

Most businesses aren't unduly unnerved by competition because it's part and parcel of their daily lives. But this particular company was unnerved. It wasn't used to the threats imposed by a competitor. Before this, its only worries had to do with customer service and market demand. Now it had to share the market.

Overnight and companywide, "competition" became a major

stressor. Management began fearing for its existence. Employees began fearing for their jobs. The firm did not know how to respond to this new and menacing stressor. Competition frightened them. And it got worse before it got better. The company almost went out of business before it turned things around and became comfortable coexisting with the new rival on the block. The ironic twist was the competition ended up being a good thing. In the long term, both companies wound up selling well more than twice the amount of the original company when it operated strictly on its own.

Sadly, the original company had to undergo a couple of very stressful years until it was able to right itself.

Had it implemented the Five Step plan in the beginning, it could have better dealt with the new stressor on the block.

First, it would have identified the stressor as "competition."

Secondly, it would have asked "Why?" and "So what?"

Thirdly, it would have uncovered the incorrect belief that was driving the neurotic, paranoid behavior causing the company to nearly go under—a belief that said, "Our value as a company is based on exclusivity of product."

Fourthly, it would have replaced the incorrect belief with a new correct belief—one that said, "Our value as a company is based on our expertise to be able to sell whatever product we choose to distribute."

Finally, it would have structured experiences (Actual, Visualized, and Modeling), so people in all facets of the company would be able to successfully imprint the new correct belief and obliterate the old incorrect belief. I would have looked to and modeled other companies that succeeded because of competition.

SCRUTINY, SCRUTINY, SCRUTINY

Whether it's personal or companywide, the questions we all want to keep asking ourselves are: "What beliefs are on my personal belief window that are incorrect?" and "How can I change them to correct beliefs?"

Since beliefs are sometimes well hidden, remember that the best way to get to the heart of our beliefs is through those things that squeak the loudest—namely, the stressors in our lives.

As we discussed earlier, a list of stressors could go on and on. We've listed just a few of them here. "Deadlines" and "moving" and "competition" are just the beginning of events that we might see as necessary stressors. We all are subject to them. If it's not traffic, it's expectations. If it's not worrying about relationships, it might be worrying about the behavior of our coworkers. It might be finances or emergencies. These stressors don't need to plague our lives, and they don't need to be altered as they're disempowered. That's the beauty of using principle-driven behavior to achieve our personal best. We don't need to change anything about the world. We don't have to eliminate anything. All we have to do is give up our old perception and replace it with a new one, based on a correct belief. Just like that, what was once a stressor won't be a stressor anymore. Whatever it was will still be on our path, exactly as it was before, but we won't look at it with fear, trepidation, anxiety, and/or loathing anymore. We'll look at it as an asset. Our obstacles will turn into stepping stones. Our deterrents will turn into encouragements.

Instant Replay

Key Points

- The quality of our life is determined by the strength of our beliefs.

- There are five steps to reversing unproductive behaviors and responses:

  (1) Identify situations that create negative emotional responses.
  (2) Ask "Why?" followed by "So what, why is that a threat?" to identify the belief and need.

(3) Identify the life experiences that created your belief.

(4) Identify a theoretical new belief or "Why Not."

(5) Structure experiences (Actual, Visualized, Modeling) to reinforce the new belief.

- Growth occurs when we apply the Five Step plan.

Personal Exercises

- Identify the recurring situations in your life (boss, deadlines, coworkers, finances) that cause negative emotional responses (frustration, anger, anxiety).

- Run these situations through the Five Step plan.

- Act on one structured experience every day for the next three weeks.

Where Do We Go from Here?

Now that we're plugged into recognizing correct beliefs, in chapter fourteen we'll look at how to refine our focus to the point where we can recognize beliefs that are even *more* correct.

CHAPTER FOURTEEN

A *More* Correct Belief

Refinement, refinement, refinement. Correct beliefs can sometimes become even *more* correct.

We've talked extensively about the need for changing incorrect beliefs to correct beliefs. It only makes sense to have beliefs in place that will drive behavior that will satisfy our needs.

Once a correct belief is in place, what then?

Then the refinement process can begin.

If the definition of a correct belief is one that meets my needs over time, then a belief that meets my needs even better over time is even *more correct*.

Life is never stagnant, and the same holds true for beliefs. Let's say, by way of example, that you have a belief on your belief window that says, "Daily exercise is important to me. It gives me the good health I need to be at my best in all my various roles."

Now you've had that belief in place long enough to determine that it is a correct belief for you. You know that because it drives behavior—an hour of exercise at least four days a week—that has produced results that over time have consistently helped you meet your needs. Because of that exercise, you enjoy general good health, your body feels fine, you're able to enjoy eating without constantly worrying about your waistline, and you have more energy for work, recreation, and family. Through exercise, you've helped satisfy your need to live, your self-worth need, your variety need, even your love need.

So you're not about to change your belief that drives your exercise behavior if you can help it. It works for you. It is correct.

NEW INFORMATION

To continue our hypothetical example, let's say that you've noticed over the past few years that more and more of the people you exercise with are occasionally leaving the aerobic workout area—your usual domain—to move into the weight room and work out with weights. Your curiosity up, you ask your friends why they're working out with weights, and they tell you that exercise physiologists have conducted a number of tests over the past few years and have discovered many of the old myths about weight lifting being of little value from a health standpoint are just that—old myths. Their research suggests that the truth of the matter is that lifting weights can be very valuable from a health standpoint. The more all of our muscles are made to work, the more our body will respond with efficient function, and the more our metabolism will increase as a result. The best general exercise program couples aerobic exercise with some kind of skeletal weight work.

But your exercise consists exclusively of the aerobic variety. Your hour of exercising consists of running or bicycling or working out on aerobic machines in the gym. Every time you exercise, you faithfully get your heart rate up to an aerobic level and keep it there throughout your workout. You do all that because of a belief on your belief window that says exercise is important to your health, and aerobic exercise is the best, most efficient form of exercise. Your heart gets a great workout, and afterward you feel great!

Now that you've heard this new information, you're confronted with a decision: Do you alter your exercise routine so it includes both aerobic work and weight work? Or do you continue as you always have, because that's worked just fine for you?

NEW AND IMPROVED

You are faced with a *more correct* belief than the one you've had in place. There wasn't anything wrong with your old belief. But now you've found a new and improved model.

Let's imagine that for years you'd walk past the weight room and dismiss weight lifting as something that was done primarily for vanity. You associated weight lifting with narcissistic behavior. Your perception was that bigger, stronger muscles didn't have much to do with good health. You never lifted weights.

Now you have new information. Now you have a decision to make. If your exercise behavior is going to include weight work, then first you're going to have to change what's on your belief window about exercise with weights.

If you go ahead and change your belief from "Daily aerobic exercise is important to my well-being" to "Daily aerobic exercise and weight work are important to my well-being" you've gone from a correct belief to a more correct belief.

At first, you'll no doubt have a difficult time combining the two kinds of exercise. For one thing, your old perceptions about weight lifting will persist. Those imprints are the result of long-developed synapses. You may not make the change at all because of these difficulties. But if you choose to develop new imprints you can. It's your choice. Gradually, the process will become easier and easier, and as a result, you will have satisfied your needs over time to an even healthier degree.

That's an easy example to see. While many other of our beliefs may not be so easy to identify, the same rules apply. Just because a belief drives behavior that meets our needs doesn't mean that belief can't be refined and altered so it drives behavior that meets our needs *even better*!

KNOWING OUR OWN BELIEFS

It's a matter of getting to know what our beliefs are. When we do that, when we really get in touch with and understand our beliefs, then we put ourselves in a position to examine them carefully and see if they can become even more correct.

I saw this evolution from correct to more correct in action recently as I worked extensively with a sales manager for a large national stockbrokerage dealership. After the sales manager became familiar with the Reality Model and the way the model helps illustrate the relationship between beliefs, behavior, and results, he decided to use the Reality Model to help the company's stockbrokers (or investment consultants) get in touch not only with the beliefs on their own personal belief windows, but also with the beliefs on the belief windows of their customers.

The company had noticed a change over the past several years in the general public's perception of "stockbrokers." A combination of aggressive marketing efforts by discount brokers, who minimize the value and importance of traditional stockbrokers, and an increasing tendency by the media to portray stockbrokers in something less than a favorable light was creating problems in the industry. As identified by national news reports and polling services, trust, it seemed, was becoming the exception, not the rule. That was the trend, and it did not look healthy.

The sales manager saw a twofold danger inherent in this lowered perception of stockbrokers: One, the public would not just regard brokers as unnecessary, but as less than honest. Two, the brokers themselves would think of their profession that way.

In other words, if either group—public or broker—bought into the belief that "Brokers are evil," well, there goes the neighborhood.

His desire was to stop any imprinting before it got out of hand. To that end, he brought all his brokers together and took them through the Reality Model just as we explained it in previous references. Then he asked each broker to evaluate his or her own beliefs and behavior. Before looking at the beliefs that drove the behavior in their professional lives, he first asked them to look at the beliefs that drove the behavior in their personal lives. This sales manager was a good salesman. He wanted them to *buy* the validity of the Reality Model, and he knew that it would be easiest for them if they first saw the connection between beliefs, behavior, and results on a personal level.

Once they could individually relate to the Reality Model, he moved into the area of professional beliefs and asked if there might be a chance that the negative campaigning currently so prevalent had diluted anyone's perception of their own profession. Had they bought into the belief that "Brokers are evil?" Was that a belief that was driving their behavior in ways that were working against them? Perhaps an unconscious behavior, but a behavior just the same, and a negative one at that.

What was their behavior saying about the beliefs on their belief windows? That's what the sales manager wanted his brokers to look at and consider.

If that behavior wasn't satisfying the necessary needs and hence reflected an incorrect belief on the belief window, he wanted his brokers to accurately identify that incorrect belief and change it to a correct belief.

"With all the negative campaigning going on," this sales manager told me, "we recognized a danger that the typical salesperson's belief window could reflect that negativity. They might not like themselves enough to be successful in selling. If you're a salesperson and you don't trust the sales profession, and that's reflected by your behavior, then that's going to come right back to you. How can you say you don't trust the sales profession and then say you trust yourself?"

The goal was to get at the root of the issue. Fix the problem, in other words, and not just the symptom. If a salesperson is only making ten calls a week, instead of the company goal of say, fifty, don't look at the behavior (making only ten calls) but instead look at the belief that is driving that behavior. What's on the salesperson's belief window that's causing the reluctance to make more calls? Find the answer and change the belief, and the calls will shoot back up to fifty.

The sales manager also spoke with his brokers about the need to get in touch with what might be on the belief windows of their customers. If a customer has been drawn into the currently popular belief that "Stockbrokers are evil" then that would explain the customer's behavior (declining interest, a tendency to shop around, a lot of hesitation, unreturned phone calls).

Going to work to help the customer change that belief would be the necessary route to try to fix the problem. Polishing and re-polishing sales approaches, or continued emphasis on the product wouldn't change anything and would only cause the broker to become more and more frustrated. Either change that belief or get a new client.

At the same time, however, the sales manager was careful to emphasize that it's important to always remember that it's only possible to have total control over your own area. He asked his brokers to ask their customers questions such as: "What do you believe about us?" "What does our behavior tell you about us?" and "What can we do better to gain your complete trust?" These questions would allow the broker to determine if there was anything the broker could do to help increase the customer's trust and improve their relationship.

"If the customer and the salesperson are operating from the same set of beliefs, then there's going to be a sound foundation of trust," he said. "And that in turn will contribute to creating an atmosphere where the customer will take an objective look at the product, as well as the broker, and not become sidetracked by anything else."

The sales manager's point is well taken. Looking at beliefs—that's what's important. For most of us, in all the areas of our lives, that means looking at our beliefs objectively and often. The world doesn't stand still, and the same applies to our beliefs. They should be constantly scrutinized and evaluated, for optimum performance.

RESULTS TELL THE TALE

In the search for more correct beliefs, it can sometimes be helpful to look at the end of the Reality Model—the Results phase. That's the phase that tells us which of the four needs are best being met. It tells us if some might be better met than others and if there's a need for any adjustment.

Think of the four needs categories that we all have. Examine them one by one: the need to live, the love need, the self-worth need, the variety need. What beliefs are on our individual belief windows that are driving the behavior that's producing the results in each of these significant areas of needs? Could any of these beliefs, even if they are correct, even if they're satisfying our needs, stand some upgrading? Some modernizing?

These are all good questions to ask. They are penetrating questions that can help us keep our beliefs in good running order.

Again, the important point to remember is that there is no right and wrong when it comes to our beliefs, only correct, incorrect, and as we're now suggesting, more correct.

The more correct beliefs will drive behavior that will better meet our needs over time.

LOOKING AT OTHER BELIEFS

One of the best ways to search for more correct beliefs is by looking at the behavior of others. Since behavior is the trail that leads to beliefs, when we see behavior that produces satisfying results in those around us, we have an opportunity to try to get in touch with the beliefs that drive that behavior.

George Plimpton, the noted "participatory author," recently wrote a book entitled *The X Factor* that I found to be a good example of "belief-probing." Plimpton's career as a journalist has been characterized by a penchant for firsthand experience. He once played a series of downs as quarterback for the Detroit Lions so he could write about what it felt like to actually play in a professional football game. For another story he put on the pads and the mask and played as a professional hockey goalie. On another occasion he got in the ring with a heavyweight boxing champion.

Through these experiences and others, George Plimpton became intrigued by an elusive, hard-to-define characteristic that seemed to be common to people the world sees as "winners."

Plimpton calls it the "X Factor." In his book he says it is common to those who greatly achieve, who "seem to be better than the sum of their parts."

What is the ingredient, he asks in the book's introduction,

> that appears to be a constant for those who are enormously successful. The "X Factor" I called it, though it is a quality which goes by many aliases: competitive spirit, the will to win, giving it 110 percent, the hidden spark, Celtic Green, Yankee pinstripes . . . guts, the killer instinct, élan vital, having the bit in one's teeth, and so on—qualities which if synthesized into a liquid form and corked up in a bottle could be sold by the millions.
>
> The X Factor is obviously of extraordinary, even morbid, interest not only to sports journalists like myself, but to general managers, coaches, athletes, and indeed the general public. What is the ingredient that makes one athlete considerably better than another, though both are of equivalent physical skills? Even more mysterious, what is it that makes an entire team better than another when the general makeup of each is about the same?

In his quest, he interviewed and/or examined people in the world of business and in the world of sports, trying to determine what set them apart. They ranged from George Bush to Vince Lombardi; to former CEOs of the H. J. Heinz Company (Anthony O'Reilly) and IBM (Thomas J. Watson, Jr.); to Bill Russell, the great basketball star. He chose these individuals because of what they had accomplished—their results—and because of the behavior they exhibited in achieving those results.

He was hot on the trail of beliefs, in other words.

In the end, Plimpton doesn't quite get there. For his purposes, his search isn't specifically to define this elusive X Factor, but to paint a word picture of those who have it.

"One of the impulses in doing this sort of research," he writes, "was that some of the X Factor ingredients might rub off on me, as well as on the reader, and that a careful reading of the text and perhaps the practice of one or two of the exercises described could result in a mild transformation. I cannot promise as much, since it hasn't happened in my case. But one can hope for the best."

GO TO THE SOURCE

The book is very entertaining, inspiring, and as it applies to the power of personal truths, extremely intriguing because of what *wasn't* explored: the beliefs adhered to by these people who found success in so many different areas of life.

Find those out, and you've found the source.

For example, to understand what drove Vince Lombardi, the great football coach and winner of numerous championships, to say "Winning isn't everything, it's the only thing," it's essential to understand what beliefs were in place on his belief window. Only by getting in touch with the very beliefs that drove his uncommon, tenacious behavior can we know why he behaved the way he did.

Indeed, the scrutiny of "great" men and women is a popular pastime for many. Biographies of people who have enjoyed great success and accomplishments are perennial best-sellers. Abraham Lincoln has been the subject of dozens of biographies or exhaustive historical probes. There is a seemingly insatiable desire to chart this great man's course, to relive his life, and perhaps to get some insight into why he was great.

Such study can be inspiring and educational. But where it can be most beneficial as it applies to our own lives is when we look beyond the behavior and look at the correct beliefs that drove that behavior.

Lincoln's life provides a good illustration of this. It is easy to sit back and admire a man who saved the union and freed the slaves, accomplishments that preserve his place in history as America's greatest president.

It's when we examine his life more carefully, when we go beyond the results and try to determine the beliefs that drove him to act the way he acted, that we can appreciate what drove him so relentlessly to his triumphs.

According to the mountains of research into his life, Lincoln seemingly behaved according to one rock-solid belief that was immovable on his belief window. He articulated that belief in his famous debates with Illinois senator Stephen A. Douglas when he said, "A house divided against itself cannot stand."

That was Lincoln's overriding belief. That was the belief that caused him to order the Union troops to stand their ground at Fort Sumter, precipitating the first armed engagement of the Civil War. Preserving the union was paramount to Lincoln. True to his strict Baptist roots, he didn't personally believe in slavery, but the moral question of slavery was not the primary issue that drove him as president of the United States. He believed, in fact, that the constitution protected slavery in the states where it already existed. But he also believed the constitution protected antislavery laws in states where they were implemented. As a result, slavery had become an issue that was dividing the union. As a president driven by a belief that the house could not be divided, Lincoln found that intolerable.

So he did everything he could to put the house back together. The end justified his means. After he became president in 1861, at a time when seven Southern states had already seceded from the union, he called every one of his chief presidential rivals to be members of his cabinet. The campaigning between these men had been bitter at times. These were men who didn't like Lincoln much, and he didn't like them; but he saw the appointments of William H. Seward as secretary of state, Salmon P. Chase as secretary of the treasury, and Edward Bates as attorney general as essential if the union was to be preserved. So that's what he did. He sacrificed his pesonal feelings to stay true to his belief.

He went to extreme lengths in his efforts to preserve the union. He suspended various civil liberties from time to time during the war, including the writ of habeas corpus. Seizing on what he saw as a constitutional loophole, he delivered the Emancipation Proclamation in 1863, an act that freed the slaves in the Confederacy because he interpreted that the constitution could only protect the rights to slavery in times of peace, not war.

In hindsight, it was clearly a stroke of genius. By the time the union had won the war, there was officially no slavery in the land. The house was no longer divided. Then the Thirteenth Amendment passed, which abolished slavery completely, ensuring that it could no longer pose a threat to divide the house.

At various junctures during this most perilous period in America's history, Lincoln's critics railed against his actions. He was called a dictator, a tyrant, an oppressor, a despot. But there was method to his madness. He was in fact none of these things. Over time, his behavior reflected that, and he enjoyed favorable results. His beliefs were correct for him and for the preserved union.

For a politican to look at the life of, say, Abraham Lincoln and benefit from his successes would be a most productive exercise. Just as it would be productive for a salesman to look at beliefs that have worked for great salesmen, or for an athlete to look at beliefs that have worked for great athletes, or for an artist to look at beliefs that have worked for great artists.

A Case of Refinement

Whatever our pursuit, there are examples to look at that can help us examine our own beliefs and see if they can become even more correct.

The distinctions can be most enlightening.

Not long ago I had occasion to work with a large real estate company. The chief broker showed me a list of his realtors and their salaries for the past year. This was a very successful company, and the salaries reflected that. The lowest salary for the previous year was just over $70,000. The highest was just over $600,000.

The chief broker said he wanted to see if he could identify the difference between that $70,000-a-year realtor and the $600,000-a-year realtor. They both worked virtually the same number of hours. They both listed approximately the same number of properties. They both had access to the same client base. From what he saw outwardly, he'd have thought they were essentially identical. But one made more than half a million dollars more than the other!

What was the difference?

Inspired by the Reality Model, he set out to determine from the behavior of these two realtors just what the beliefs were on their respective belief windows—beliefs that drove one to behave to the tune of $70,000 a year in commissions and the other to behave to the tune of $600,000 a year in commissions.

What he discovered I found to be most enlightening. He found that the $70,000-a-year realtor had a belief that said you had to do everything perfectly. You had to dot every *i* and cross every *t*. No detail was too small to be overlooked.

Conversely, he found that the $600,000-a-year realtor had a belief that said it was OK to skip the small stuff. Details didn't matter as much as results.

The realtor on the low-end was actually being hampered by a belief of perfectionism. That was what was bogging down the process. In the business of selling real estate, it was a detriment if you were too efficient. Too much focus on every detail could greatly inhibit your success.

The broker's goal was to consider how to effectively communicate that message to the $70,000-a-year realtor. If that realtor—not exactly a failure by anyone's standards—could alter his belief to a more correct belief, it could result in a dramatic change in income.

WE'RE IN CONTROL

In the final analysis, the point is that it's important to realize that we're in control of our beliefs, and not vice versa. They can be altered, adjusted, amended, revised. They *can* be changed when it makes sense to change them, when it means behavior that will better produce results that meet our needs over time.

When a *correct* belief meets a *more correct* belief, it only makes sense to adjust and adopt the belief that is more correct.

There is a classic story I'd like to relate that sums up what I'm trying to say. It involves a navy captain aboard an aircraft carrier. The carrier is underway in the ocean, going full steam. It's night, and all the ship's lights are on, when the captain sees, off in the distance on the horizon, another light.

He gets on the radio.

"Attention," he calls out. "We are on a collision course. Change your course 30 degrees."

"I suggest that you change your course 30 degrees instead," comes the reply.

"I'm a captain, and I'm ordering you to change your course," indignantly responds the captain.

"I'm a seaman first class and I still suggest that you change your course," comes the reply.

By now incensed by this insolence, the captain plays his hole card and responds authoritatively, "We are a battleship."

To which the seaman replies, "We are a lighthouse."

A correct belief was about to meet a more correct belief, and the captain adjusted accordingly.

Instant Replay

Key Points

- We can have personal breakthroughs by replacing correct beliefs with *more* correct beliefs.

- Studying the lives of successful people helps us identify the more correct beliefs we can apply in our lives.

Personal Exercises

- Identify areas of your life that you would like to take to a higher level.

- Model your life after someone who is already at a higher level to identify a more correct belief and how to implement it.

Where Do We Go from Here?

In chapter fifteen, I'd like to share a number of success stories. I've seen this "power" drive meaningful growth in many lives, particularly my own.

Change Happens

It really does! My life changed through the power of beliefs, and I've seen countless others reflect this change in their lives as well.

Whenever I'm asked what it is that drives my fervor for the meaningful changes that can come into our lives through adopting new beliefs, my answer is always the same: My enthusiasm comes from personal experience. I have seen meaningful change happen in my own life, and I have seen it happen in the lives of many others. I have seen it work! Seeing lives change for the better, through the application of correct individual beliefs, is a thrilling experience and one that never gets old. For that reason, my enthusiasm has only increased over the years.

Of course these experiences are not unique to me. Franklin Covey "change trainers" all around the country and the world also constantly have the opportunity to witness meaningful change when people discover what's really driving them. Many of these trainers' experiences and personal stories have already been shared in the pages of this book, and they're just the tip of the iceberg. They are merely representative of thousands of others, all attesting to the power of beliefs to initiate the changes that lead us to achieve our personal best.

CHANGES EVERYWHERE

The changes the trainers and I have seen come in all areas and walks of life. Often, even though the original emphasis is on job satisfaction and performance, the changes that take place are far afield from the workplace. There was the case of one employee in a company in the Midwest who, after learning about the Reality Model and the benefits that result when correct beliefs drive behavior, took his newfound tools to the aid of his teenage son, an eighth-grader who was having difficulties in the classroom. It seemed that very early in his schooling the son had been tagged by child psychologists as a "slow learner." Although there was no hard evidence to support the slow-learner theory, the news nonetheless got through loud and clear to the son, who dutifully imprinted that message and labeled himself as a "slow learner." Consequently, his grades and classroom performance in general were quite poor and showed no sign of changing.

The boy's father decided to use the Reality Model as a vehicle to help his son understand what was driving his poor classroom behavior. He and his wife sat down with their son and patiently drew out the Reality Model, starting with the Needs Wheel and continuing through the Belief Window, the Rules, the Behavior, the Results, and the timeline connecting Results back to the Needs Wheel. They explained to their son how our behavior is the direct result of the beliefs we've put on our belief windows, and how the results of our behavior reflect those beliefs. They further explained how important it is to analyze the results of our behavior in connection with our needs. If our needs are being met, then the results are a product of behavior being driven by beliefs that are correct for us. If our needs are not being met, on the other hand, then the results are a product of behavior being driven by beliefs that are incorrect for us.

For the first time, by utilizing the Reality Model, both the parents and the teenage son looked realistically at what was driving the behavior of this eighth-grade student. They realized he had a belief that said he couldn't do well in school because he was a "slow learner." As long as he kept that belief, it would stay on his belief window, and his behavior would translate into results that would reinforce the image he had of himself as a "slow learner." The problem was, his self-worth need was taking a beating as a result. And his grades weren't looking too good, either.

If new imprinting could take place and create a new belief that said, "I am not a slow learner. If I study, concentrate, and work hard I can be successful in the classroom," the results could reflect a completely different kind of behavior and, when analyzed, could show success at meeting the teenager's self-worth need.

A SUCCESSFUL CHANGE OF BELIEF

Such imprinting did take place. The family, in effect, went through the Five Step plan. They identified the stressor and asked "Why?" and "So what?" They identified where the incorrect belief came from, came up with a theoretical new belief, and structured experiences to imprint that new principle. As a result, a "good learner" was born out of what had been labeled a "slow learner."

That trainer's experience served to reinforce something that had been impressed upon me over and over again during my competitive athletic career: People categorize themselves and then stay in that category by habit. Race after race and year after year I noticed this phenomenon. As I've discussed earlier, more often than not, runners would finish where they thought they should finish. I remember how much this worked to my advantage—quite inadvertently I might add—when I was trying to make my fourth United States Olympic team at the Olympic Track and Field Trials in the summer of 1988.

I had come down with a case of pneumonia prior to the meet and was barely getting better by the time of my semifinal race. I needed to place in the top six to be able to move on to the finals—no small task, I knew, under the circumstances.

Trying to conserve my energy, I ran as easily as I could with an eye not on winning the semifinal but on making it into the top six. All was going well enough until the final lap, when a runner passing me on the inside while jumping over a barrier cut too close and knocked me down. As I fell to the track I stuck my hand out to cushion the blow, when the runner in front of me accidentally caught my hand with the spikes on the bottom of his shoe. I was bleeding and flat out on the track—and by now a good twenty yards behind the field, with only 200 yards to the finish line.

That's when my expectations took over and, I have to believe, when the expectations of those I was running against also took over. I was an eight-time national champion. I knew it. They knew it. I *thought* I'd place in the top six. They thought I'd place in the top six. I got to my feet and did what we all thought I'd do. I made up those twenty yards, passing just enough runners to finish, you guessed it, in sixth place. In the finals two days later, with the cut in my hand stitched, I was able to qualify for the Seoul Olympics.

There is another example of two mid-level executives who made what some would consider rather drastic changes while being trained in this material. Their company was going through a reengineering overhaul, and as you might imagine there was a lot of soul-searching going on as to the changes inherent with that reengineering. Both executives were faced with "Is this what I want to do with my life?" questions.

DIFFERENT ANSWERS

They wound up answering them in different ways. One decided to switch to part-time status with the company and the other decided to leave entirely. Neither decision was based on a dissatisfaction with the new direction the company was heading, however. Instead, each decision was based on values and needs. Both of these executives took a good, honest look at what they wanted most in life and acted upon what they saw.

The executive who switched to part-time status did so because he realized he wanted to devote more time to his wife and family—areas he felt he had neglected for too long. He turned down an opportunity to become a chief player in the company's reengineering because along with the promotion would come longer working hours and an increased workload. He was in a position where he could still provide for his family financially while at the same time cutting back on his company involvement. Because his value system placed a premium on his family relationships, and because he sensed a need to place more of an emphasis in terms of time and energy in that area, he made a *meaningful change* in his life that would better satisfy his needs.

The executive who left the company entirely also turned down what would have been a promotion in the reengineering process. He elected instead to pursue a goal he'd had in the back of his mind for several years, playing on the professional Senior Golf Tour. He assessed his situation and decided he was financially well equipped to be able to take two years off for intensive practice, after which he'd go out and give the tour a shot. There was no guarantee that he'd be successful as a professional golfer, but he had the full-fledged support and encouragement of his spouse and family, who all agreed that the satisfaction was going to be in the trying. He didn't have to make it; all he had to do was give it his best and enjoy the process. With all that support behind his pursuit, he turned in his notice at work and then went to work on his short game.

In this example, neither executive had a problem with his job. Both had performed long enough and well enough that they were in a position for excellent promotions. They each also realized upon reflection that there were other values in their lives that also had meaning. By putting the right beliefs in place, change wasn't difficult. Quite the opposite was true. Change was welcomed.

GIVE IT TIME

Helping people get in touch with those meaningful values is what's at the heart of my work. After being introduced to the Reality Model and the concept of achieving one's personal best by implementing correct beliefs, people are asked to incorporate into their lives their chosen "new" beliefs, for twenty-one days—enough time to formulate new habits. After those twenty-one days, they are asked to write me a letter, articulating the results and what they might mean.

Those twenty-one-day letters provide a constant stream of positive reinforcement that behavior based on correct beliefs indeed changes people's lives and helps them achieve new personal bests. The most gratifying part of my profession is seeing people lead happier, healthier, and more productive lives as a result of applying these concepts in their lives.

Let's look at another example to further illustrate. This story comes from a company on the West Coast and involves a woman in her early forties who had been a legal secretary most of her working life. She had an affinity for the law and was in high demand as a secretary, often doing the same research and document preparation as the lawyers she worked for.

For years this secretary had squelched a desire to become an attorney because of all the reasons you might imagine. She was too old, she had a family to care for—those were two of the reasons. And of course there was the big one—that she was a woman!

That last reason she didn't precisely articulate to herself. It was an imprint, an unconscious yet very powerful belief. She had grown up in a home with an authoritative father who, while kind and gentle in most ways, was very much a male chauvinist. He was a banker, and at his bank all the managers were men and all the tellers, as well as the secretaries, were women. He did not encourage his daughter to go to college, although her brothers were encouraged to get their degrees. He did not encourage his daughter to forge a professional career. He encouraged her to be a homemaker, like her mother, or, at the very most, a secretary. This woman had been raised by a staunch traditionalist.

So that was her imprint, and it created a strong belief that said, "Women are subservient to men." She carried that belief onto her belief window, which drove her behavior to become a secretary and to remain a secretary.

This woman wasn't driven to change by participating in my seminar, however. Her process of changing beliefs was much like mine when I left the law—she did it on her own. When the pain got great enough for her she did something about it. Her pain came in the form of seeing lawyers make considerably more money than she did every payday, even though they performed many of the same tasks and worked the same number of hours. Comparing a $15-an-hour secretary's pay to a $125-an-hour lawyer's pay is painful in its own way. Her pain also came in the dull ache she constantly felt in knowing she was stifling her potential.

So she went to law school. She was the oldest person in her class. And the smartest. She sacrificed some things in her life during her three years of law school and put other things on hold, but when the three years were up—and the time went faster than she imagined it would—she had her diploma. She was a card-carrying member of the bar. The firm that valued her services so much as a secretary hired her first as a clerk, then as an associate, and before long she became a partner in the firm. The new belief on her belief window—"Women can perform tasks equally as well as men"—had driven her to a change that was very significant and meaningful in her life.

CHANGE DOESN'T HAVE TO BE EXTREME

Such success stories are heartwarming and serve as excellent examples for others to follow. I always like to throw out a caution, however, that examples of extreme career changes shouldn't mislead us into thinking that change has to mean drastic and dramatic leaps. Many times a realistic look at our beliefs allows us to be content with our current circumstances. Or it might prod us to effect change that is less dramatic than a wholesale change of career or environment. Subtle change is effective, too. Sometimes it's the minor adjustments that make all the difference.

For instance, working at what might be considered an entry-level job can nonetheless be quite fulfilling and satisfying for the person who has a large family to care for and recognizes the value of having the employment. If our correct beliefs are in place, paying dues becomes much easier to do. We're willing to be patient and put up with more because of the knowledge we have inside that our needs will be best met over time.

Besides generating meaningful change, a clear understanding of the power of our beliefs also helps make us aware of the physiological occurrences that take place in our lives as we deal with the various mental obstacles and threats that constantly appear. When we realize that our bodies generate toxins, for example, after cortisol is released during vigilant responses, we also realize we must disperse those toxins through physical exertion. Many trainers I've worked with have had experiences with people who credit this awareness with literally saving their lives.

When we know what's going on, in other words, we then put ourselves in a position to do something about it. All of the preventive medicine measures, such as exercise, financial planning, time management, and relationship skills, take on more real significance. All of a sudden "going to the gym" has more incentive behind it than simply "I gotta work on the old waistline." All of a sudden sitting down and working out a financial budget that concentrates on spending less than you make is a worthwhile exercise. All of a sudden planning a trip to Yosemite with your spouse "just to see the falls we've always wanted to see" makes perfect sense. All of a sudden making time for a trek in the Himalayas isn't so selfish and self-centered after all.

That's because we are in touch with our beliefs, which means we're in touch with ourselves, and the tremendous part about that is that we finally have total control of ourselves.

THE CONCEPT OF "OVER TIME"

Correct beliefs give us the energy, the stamina, the enthusiasm, to go on with what's important to us in our lives, to keep striving. Correct beliefs give us the concept of "over time." Correct beliefs enable us to quit sacrificing what we want most for what we want now.

Without a correct belief on my personal belief window I am convinced I would have quit track and field after the 1984 Olympic Games. When the Olympic medal I had been pursuing most of my life landed just out of my grasp, I truly believe I would have packed it in then and there if my behavior had still been driven by the belief that my success and self-worth were dependent upon beating other people and winning medals.

Luckily, my personal finish line was internal, and I was able to absorb the disappointment as a personal triumph. I felt good about giving that Olympic race everything I had. I felt a sense of personal peace and calm.

That peace and calm not only enabled me to continue on as a competitor, but to thrive. By the time the 1985 season began and the virus had mercifully run its course—although it would persist throughout the rest of my career—I was ready to go. I participated in the usual early season meets, finding my competitive legs once again. By the time the national championships came along I was in good enough shape to capture my eighth straight national steeplechase title. By the fall of that season, after months of serious training, I was able to achieve what for me were two significant personal goals. The first came in Bern, Switzerland, when I ran a sub-four-minute mile for the first time in my life. I know, I was a steeplechaser, and steeplechasers aren't milers, but since my goals were set inwardly, that accomplishment meant a great deal to me even if the world took absolutely no notice. My achievement of that "milestone" of breaking the four-minute barrier was personally very gratifying.

The second significant goal was realized in August of 1985 in Koblenz, Germany. I was determined to not only lower my own American steeplechase record that night on the track, but break the 8:10 barrier as well—a barrier that, to that point in time, had been broken by only four other runners.

As I previously related, I visualized that night's race all during the afternoon, programming in my mind the exact pace I needed to run. The existing American record, as well as my personal best time, was an 8:12.37 I had run in 1983, so I knew I had my work cut out for me. Two and a half seconds is a relative eternity in a 3,000-meter race. But I was determined, and in my own mind I felt I was ready. Since the Olympic "disappointment" a year ago, I had trained better than anytime in my life.

The race went like (pardon the expression) clockwork. I hit every split right on and then, on the gun lap, found a little extra. I'd found that two and a half seconds and a little to spare. I finished in 8:09.17.

I placed first in eleven of the twelve races I entered in 1985. In the twelfth race, which took place in Australia, I got out leaned at the tape after having just made a trip from European competitions. It was the best year I'd ever enjoyed during my steeplechasing career, and it came after what most people saw as my biggest disappointment. I know I couldn't have kept running at such a high level if every time I walked onto a track I dwelled on how unfair life had been to me at the Olympic Games of 1984 and that I was somehow a failure because I had been beaten by other people.

My principle of not quitting until I'd given my best drove me to a long and satisfying running career—one that included a top ten world ranking for twelve straight years and the second highest number of ranking points ever accumulated by a steeplechaser (one point behind Bronislaw Malinowski of Poland, the gold-medal winner of the 1980 Moscow Olympic Games). I started to gradually slow down after 1985 but, still, there was another Olympic Games on the horizon in Seoul, South Korea, in 1988, and I determined that I wanted to make that my curtain call. I trained accordingly and at the age of thirty-four wound up placing sixth in an Olympic final that turned out to be the fastest steeplechase race ever. I remember the emotion I felt when that race was over. I was satisfied I had done what I'd promised myself that day many years ago in Provo, Utah, when I returned to the BYU track long enough "to see how far I could go, to see just what I could do." Before I left the Olympic stadium I knelt down and kissed the track good-bye. Most of the 80,000 people in the stands either took no notice or wondered what on earth that American who finished sixth was doing kissing the track. I wasn't the winner in their minds. But thankfully, I was in mine.

Appendix

NEEDS ASSESSMENT

UNDERSTANDING YOUR NEEDS: A SELF TEST

Circle the number that best describes you today.

		Strongly Agree	_	_	_	Strongly Disagree
A1.	I have someone in whom I can trust or confide safely, without judgment.	5	4	3	2	1
A2.	I have supportive friends on whom I can depend.	5	4	3	2	1
A3.	I feel loved and wanted, that people genuinely like me as a person.	5	4	3	2	1
A4.	My need for intimacy (emotional and physical) is filled to my satisfaction.	5	4	3	2	1
A5.	I like myself.	5	4	3	2	1

A ☐

B6.	I enjoy the people with whom I work.	5	4	3	2	1
B7.	I feel accepted by my work group.	5	4	3	2	1

		5	4	3	2	1
B8.	I provide help and support to coworkers.	5	4	3	2	1
B9.	I feel I am making a positive contribution through my job to the lives of other people.	5	4	3	2	1
B10.	I feel my colleagues trust me.	5	4	3	2	1

B ☐

		5	4	3	2	1
C11.	I am satisfied with my present health and fitness.	5	4	3	2	1
C12.	I live and work in a safe environment.	5	4	3	2	1
C13.	I feel good about my future.	5	4	3	2	1
C14.	I feel in control financially.	5	4	3	2	1
C15.	I have resources to fall back on (i.e., finances, family support, job skills) should my present circumstances change for the worse.	5	4	3	2	1

C ☐

		5	4	3	2	1
D16.	I feel my job is secure.	5	4	3	2	1
D17.	I feel comfortable with how my work is evaluated.	5	4	3	2	1
D18.	My professional routine positively impacts my physical health.	5	4	3	2	1
D19.	I have skills that are valuable/in demand in the job marketplace.	5	4	3	2	1
D20.	I feel that the policies and norms of the organization I work for protect my interests.	5	4	3	2	1

D ☐

E21.	I feel good about where I am in life and where I am headed.	5	4	3	2	1
E22.	I feel that people value my ideas and opinions highly.	5	4	3	2	1
E23.	I feel a sense of purpose in my life, that I really matter.	5	4	3	2	1
E24.	I feel others confide in me.	5	4	3	2	1
E25.	I feel I am growing and improving myself.	5	4	3	2	1

E ☐

F26.	My work is regarded highly by my colleagues.	5	4	3	2	1
F27.	I feel my efforts at work contribute significantly to what the organization is all about.	5	4	3	2	1
F28.	I feel I have influence among my colleagues.	5	4	3	2	1
F29.	I feel confident in my ability to contribute at work.	5	4	3	2	1
F30.	I feel positive about the direction of my career.	5	4	3	2	1

F ☐

G31.	I really enjoy my life.	5	4	3	2	1
G32.	I regularly spend time doing things that are really important to me.	5	4	3	2	1
G33.	I feel comfortable with the amount of discretionary time in my life.	5	4	3	2	1

G34. I feel comfortable expressing   5   4   3   2   1
and sharing the uniqueness
of my personality.

G35. I rarely feel trapped or   5   4   3   2   1
without options.

G ☐

H36. I find my job interesting   5   4   3   2   1
and stimulating.

H37. I am reaching my potential   5   4   3   2   1
in my career.

H38. I feel my job is free of drudgery   5   4   3   2   1
or monotony.

H39. I feel my workplace permits a   5   4   3   2   1
comfortable amount of flexibility
in policy and procedure.

H40. I take enough breaks and   5   4   3   2   1
vacations from my work routine.

H ☐

RETHINKING STRESS, UNDERSTANDING YOUR STRESS

SCORING:

1. Total your circled responses in each group of the five and place the number in the lettered box.

2. Plot the numbers in their respective sections of the Needs Wheel below. Each concentric circle represents 5 points.

3. Draw a continuous line between each of your plotted points to make a circle shape.

4. Total the scores of all boxes and place in the Composite Score box below. This score indicates your overall susceptibility to stress. The higher the score (200 = highest possible), the less frequently common stressors are likely to "get to you."

COMPOSITE SCORE

This chart represents your Needs Wheel. The areas where your Needs Wheel is "flat" indicate areas where your needs are not being met to your satisfaction. This is NOT a psychological profile, nor is it intended to be used as such. It is only a nonscientific attempt to help you discover the strengths and weaknesses of your Needs Wheel.

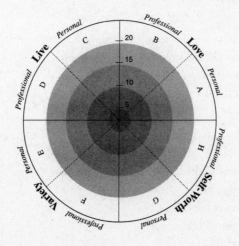

YOUR HUMOR QUOTIENT

Laughter is food for the soul—and every other part of the human body. Even if the healing effects of chuckling have not been documented by numerous contemporary "experts," our instincts tell us it feels good to smile and appreciate the lighter moments in life. Evaluate your potential for effective humor-coping skills below:

I laugh at least ___times a day.
    a. more than 20 (5 points)___points
    b. 10–20 (4)
    c. 5–10 (2)
    d. 5 or fewer (1)

I love to "belly laugh" and share open humor.
    a. almost always (5 points)___points
    b. most of the time (4)
    c. sometimes (3)
    d. seldom (2)
    e. never (1)

I feel I have a great sense of humor.
    a. most of the time (5 points)___points
    b. sometimes (3)
    c. not really (1)

Family, friends, and coworkers think I have a great sense of humor.
    a. most of the time (5 points)___points
    b. often (4)
    c. sometimes (3)
    d. seldom (2)
    e. hardly ever (1)

I tend to view life pretty seriously.
   a. less than 20–30 percent (5 points)____points
   b. about half the time (3)
   c. 80–90 percent of the time (1)

Your Total:____

Coping Effectiveness Scale:
Low   Average   High
05–10   15–20   25–30

Printed with permission from the Institute of Stress Medicine, 1989.

Exercise Log

Day	Date	Exercise Type	Minutes Warm-up	Minutes Exercise	Minutes Cool-Down	Distance (Optional)	Target Heart Rate (10 secs.)	Weight (pounds)	Comments	Points
1										
2										
3										
4										
5										
6										
7										
8										
9										
10										
11										
12										
13										
14										
15										
16										
17										
18										
19										
20										
21										
22										
23										
24										
25										
26										
27										
28										
29										
30										
31										
32										
33										

Fitness Institute L.D.S. Hospital S.L.C., Utah

Resting Heart Rate (60 secs.) _____

Date _____

CL 4058

Personal Food Record

If you are having trouble finding where those additional calories come from or can't tell if you are eating low-fat, healthful choices, keep track of your daily food intake for a few days.

*Hungry
Anxious
Lonely
Tired

Date	Time	Food	% of Fat	Calories	Alternative Food	Reason* Hunger/ Other	

Do You Eat to Live or Live to Eat?

Index

Index

About the Author

Henry Marsh became the second American male runner to make four U.S. Olympic track teams in 1988. His career culminated with thirteen straight years as one of the top ten 3,000-meter steeplechase runners in the world—three years as number one. He has also held the American record for an unprecedented eighteen years in a row. During that time, Henry graduated cum laude in economics from BYU and received his law degree from the University of Oregon.

After practicing law with the Salt Lake City firm of Parsons, Behle & Latimer, Henry became a consultant for the Franklin Covey Company. There, he developed curriculum for increasing personal and professional productivity, which has been used by corporations throughout the United States and Canada.

Henry has traveled more than a million miles as a seminar presenter, a speaker, and a lecturer. He addresses thousands every year at businesses, sales organizations, and schools. Additionally, he has certified hundreds of trainers in his and other Franklin Covey courses to teach in their respective companies.

About Franklin Covey Co.

Franklin Covey Co. is a 4,500-member international firm devoted to helping individuals, organizations, and families become more effective. Franklin Covey Co. is the leading global provider of integrated, sustainable professional services and product solutions based on proven principles. The company's client portfolio includes eighty-two of the Fortune 100 companies, more than two-thirds of the Fortune 500 companies, as well as thousands of small and midsize companies, and government entities, educational institutions, communities, families, and millions of individual consumers. Franklin Covey Co. has also created pilot partnerships with cities seeking to become principle-centered communities, and is currently teaching the 7 Habits to teachers and administrators in more than 4,500 schools and universities nationwide and through statewide initiatives with education leaders in twenty-seven states.

The vision of Franklin Covey Co. is to teach people to teach themselves and become independent of the company. To the timeless adage by Lao-tzu; "Give a man a fish and you feed him for a day; teach him how to fish and you feed him for a lifetime," they add, "Develop teachers of fishermen, and you lift all society." This empowerment process is carried out through programs conducted at facilities in the Rocky Mountains of Utah, custom consulting services, personal coaching, custom on-site training, and client-facilitated training, as well as through open-enrollment workshops offered in more than 500 cities in North America and forty countries worldwide.

With more than 19,000 licensed client facilitators teaching its curriculum within their organizations, Franklin Covey Co. trains in excess of 750,000 participants annually. Implementation tools, including the Franklin Planner and a wide offering of audio and videotapes, books, and computer software programs, enable clients to retain and effectively utilize concepts and skills. These and other products carefully selected and endorsed by Franklin Covey Co. are available in more than 130 Franklin Covey Stores throughout North America and in several other countries.

Franklin Covey Co. products and materials are now available in thirty-two languages, and their planner products are used by more than fifteen million individuals worldwide. The company has more than fifteen million books in print, with more than one and a half million sold each year.

For information on the Franklin Covey Store or International Office closest to you, or for a free catalog of Franklin Covey products and programs, call or write:

Franklin Covey Company
2200 West Parkway Boulevard
Salt Lake City, Utah 84119-2331 USA
Toll Free: 800-827-1776
Fax: 801-496-4252
International callers: 801-229-1333 or fax 801-229-1233
Internet: http://www.franklincovey.com

Franklin Covey's products and programs provide a wide range of resources for individuals and families, and business, government, nonprofit, and education organizations, including:

Programs

Leadership Week	The Power Principle
Principle-Centered Leadership	Planning for Results
The 7 Habits of Highly Effective People	Presentation Advantage
	Writing Advantage
What Matters Most Time Management	Building Trust
	Getting to Synergy

About Franklin Covey Co.

The Power of Understanding
Facilitator Workshops for In-
    House Certification

Products

Franklin Planner
Ascend Franklin Day Planner
    software
TimeQuest self-paced video
    workshop
First Things First self-paced
    video workshop
7 Habits audio tapes
Living the 7 Habits audio tapes
Principle-Centered Leadership
    audio tapes
First Things First audio tapes
7 Habits of Highly Effective
    Families audio tapes
How to Write a Family Mission
    Statement audio tapes
Balancing Work and Family
    audio tapes
The Power Principle audio
    tapes
7 Habits Effectiveness Profile
Stakeholder Information
    System (SIS) Baseline
    Report
Franklin Covey Leadership
    Library video workshops
7 Habits poster series

Custom Consulting and Speeches

Custom Principle-Centered
    Leadership Programs
Custom On-Site Programs
Consulting and Speeches
Keynote Addresses
Custom Education Programs

Publications

Priorities Magazine
*The 7 Habits of Highly Effective
    People*
*The 10 Natural Laws of
    Successful Time and Life
    Management*
Principle-Centered Leadership
First Things First
The Power Principle
To Do . . . Doing . . . Done
First Things First Every Day
*Daily Reflections of Highly
    Effective People*
Franklin Covey Style Guide
*The 7 Habits of Highly Effective
    Families*
*The 7 Habits of Highly Effective
    Teens*
The Nature of Leadership